Our Sacred Garden

THE LIVING EARTH

Reuniting us with Nature

by Adele Seronde

SANCTUARY PUBLICATIONS

Our Sacred Garden: The Living Earth

Published by Sanctuary Publications, Inc.

P.O. Box 20697, Sedona, AZ 86341

All paintings and poetry are by Adele Seronde, unless otherwise indicated. The paintings on the divider pages are as follows: Azalea Summer, page 1; Lupine, page 55; Transformation, page 91; Fire Wheel, page 140; and The Guardians, page 171.

OTHER BOOKS BY ADELE SERONDE

Children's phonetic poetry books, Wenkart Publishing Co.: "Ask a Daffodil," 1967 and "Ask a Cactus Rose," 1971.

"Deliver Into Green," Wampeter Press (poetry), 1982.

Co-authored with "Wordwatchers," Sedona, AZ: "Between Silences," 1990; "Facets," 1999; "Aria," 2000.

ACKNOWLEDGMENTS

I would like to thank the members of my family and numerous friends who have given time, advice, commentaries and exchange of ideas. They are my sons and daughters; my grandson Michael Seronde; my nephew Eric and his wife Hoa Herter; niece Caroline Herter; and friends Erma Pounds, Mimi Griffin Crowell, Thistle Brown, Page Bryant, Daniel J. Finn, Katherine D. Kane, Jack Powers, Julie Stone, Vijali Hamilton, Eugenia Everett, Millie Chapin, Aya (Jean-Marie Schiff), Lane Badger, Joanna Crell, Lily Yeh, Ani Williams, Judith Quarrington; Jerry Simmons for his excellent advice; Catherine Rourke, Eveline Horelle Dailey and Rosemary Licher; Jane Perini for designing the book and Wib Middleton for photographing my artwork.

Most of all I am grateful to my courageous editors, James Bishop, Jr., and Bennie Blake; and finally, to Carol Horn for her endless patience, good will and advice.

I dedicate this book to my children,

Antoine, Jacques, Pierre, Dorée, Jeanne

and to my whole and extended family

as well as to my beloved deceased parents and husband.

CONTENTS

PROLOGUE   7

PREFACE   9

PART I   What Are Sacred Gardens?   13

Chapter One   MEANINGS OF "SACRED"   14

Chapter Two   PERSONAL AWAKENING TO THE SACRED   26

Chapter Three   THE NEED FOR GARDENS MADE SACRED BY LOVE   40

Chapter Four   THE METAPHYSICS OF SACRED GARDENS   50

Chapter Five   THE CHALICE GARDEN   60

PART II   Healing of Community   67

Chapter Six   URBAN GARDENS AND PLAYGROUNDS   68

Chapter Seven   VISIONARIES AND TRANSFORMERS   78

Chapter Eight   LILY YEH—THE VILLAGE OF ARTS & HUMANITIES   90

PART III Healing of the Whole Earth   101

Chapter Nine   AWAKENING THE VISIONARY IN ALL OF US   102

Chapter Ten   PROTECTING THE GARDEN OF THE EARTH   122

Chapter Eleven   PASSIVE AND ACTIVE HEALING   128

Chapter Twelve   GARDENS FOR HUMANITY   136

PART IV Voices of the Future   151

Chapter Thirteen   VISIONARY VOICES   152

Chapter Fourteen   HOW PEOPLE ARE MEETING THE CHALLENGES   158

Final Words   179

CONCLUSION   180

EPILOGUE   183

APPENDIX   185

BIBLIOGRAPHY   190

ABOUT THE AUTHOR   192

PROLOGUE

BECOMING

Once people said I was a Diva
  to a world of plants.
They said I would take this flower
  of my green volition
  and inseminate the world!

So I must offer
  soon
a resolution made of green
in multiple tones of song.

I must weave cantatas of bulrushes
  bent in wind—
  strains of catkins
  grass-head seeds and sky
to wrap this dying world
  and me—in soul-heat–
infuse us with a solar passion so intense
we are in symphonic presence
  of becoming.

Aspen Garden

PREFACE

A visit to the Chalice Well Garden in Glastonbury, England, decades ago, turned out to be the incentive for writing this book. This garden brings seekers from all over the world, who believe that Jesus came there to be taught the wisdom of the Druids. They are blessed by the waters of the Chalice Well. I went to the well-head by myself. In the silence and beauty, I was overwhelmed by a desire to dedicate my life to listening to the cries of our suffering Earth and offering whatever solace I could in the form of gardens. Each one has become part of *Our Sacred Garden: The Living Earth.*

I believe that the planting of gardens, both in the soil and in the heart, is one deeply creative and healing action which can enchant people of any culture, race, or belief. Indeed, the garden is a metaphor for healing both self and community. It is the exploration of the symbolic Sacred Garden; the original paradise of everyone's dream; that place of lost myth and poetry, so needed today; a sanctuary of healing, color, and fragrances, of still and running waters; a source of fresh resolution in our hands and in ourselves by which we can transform the planet.

In retrospect, art and gardens and family have always been my life. Around me, I have always had the music, colors and fragrances of gardens. As a painter, shapes, lines and color are my language, weaving together a tapestry of living greens, flames, sapphires and prisms. Happiness, to me, is emerald and viridian; anger, a striated crimson; and inspiration, scarlet and gold.

At the age of three, I was kneeling with paper and crayons on the outdoor steps of our house in

*To forget how
to dig the earth
and to tend the soil
is to forget ourselves.*
Mahatma Gandhi

The many great gardens of the world, of literature and poetry, of painting and music, of religion and architecture, all make the point as clear as possible: The soul cannot thrive in the absence of a garden.
THOMAS MOORE

Boston. It was Thanksgiving Day. A huge inflated float of a pilgrim was being carried down Beacon Hill in front of us. "Turn around!" cried my family. I wouldn't, as I was much too busy, finally able to draw the sideburns of a little boy. I had attempted this for days. Before long, drawing was my everyday life, along with radio and homework. Drawing portraits of teachers, fellow students and innumerable horses was more fun than boring classes at school.

Like a thunderclap, the shock of real art arrived when I saw my first prints by Braque, Picasso and Miro in my parent's house in Washington, D.C. It was a jolt of pure pleasure when I realized what those artists were sharing with me. Soon thereafter, in the Boston Museum of Fine Arts, there was Renoir's "Dancers" in his world of dazzling color and light. After that, I proceeded on a journey through the eyes of Monet, Pizarro, and more Renoirs and on to the genius of Gauguin and Van Gogh. Now, some 60 years later, I recognize that my whole life has been inspired by spiritual lightning that caused me to absorb those avatars of form and color.

Down through the decades, I've learned that we can translate the meaning of gardens into our daily lives as places of inner radiance in our minds and hearts. We can nurture gardens of our soul and create places in which to build communities around planning, planting, and maintaining physical gardens.

Hopefully, this book will light the way for all of us.

– Adele Seronde

SOUTHWEST CORONATION

11

*Your sacred
space is where
you can find
yourself again
and again.*

JOSEPH CAMPBELL

What Are Sacred Gardens?

CHAPTER ONE

Meanings of "Sacred"

The land of Uttarakura is watered by lakes with golden lotuses.
There are rivers by thousands, full of leaves of the color of sapphire and lapis lazuli;
and the lakes, resplendent like the morning sun, are adorned by golden beds of red lotus.
The country all around is covered by jewels and precious stones, with gay beds of blue lotus,
golden petalled. Instead of sand, pearls, gems and gold form the banks of the rivers,
which are overhung with trees of fire-bright gold. These trees perpetually bear
flowers and fruit, give forth a sweet fragrance and abound with birds.

– From the *Ramayana,* one of two great Indian epics, circa 1000 BCE

What does this term "sacred" mean to me, to any of us who may, or may not, worship in a formal way? What does it mean to those of us who perceive the language of the Spirit in the stained-glass windows of Chârtres or Notre Dame, or in Beethoven's Ninth Symphony? And what about those who find majesty in the great redwood forests, in the waterfalls, the mountains and on the grass-blown prairies?

Early morning light at Stonehenge, located in the English county of Wiltshire.

Assuredly, one meaning of "sacred" is a person's awareness of the reverence in the journey through life to find the soul's domain, the life force or energy of God by whatever name. Similar journeys are immortalized in the world's greatest literature: Arjuna's battles in the *Bhagavad-Gita*, the enlightenment of Buddha, Noah's Ark in the Bible, and the wanderings of Moses, his receiving of the Ten Commandments, and safeguarding them in the Ark of the Covenant.

Entering the 21st century, are we still haunted by the symbolism of the Holy Grail? Do we have Parsivals among us today? Sailing countless miles into space, did not at least some of the astronauts see our planet of swirling blues and greens as a spiritual miracle of existence? This search for sacred gardens continues. To some seekers it means a blessed sanctuary or oasis, a cloister connected to a church or a monastery, a consecrated haven secure from violation. To others it may be a garden that's always been dedicated to a spiritual energy in a site proclaimed as holy by a shaman, Druid or priest. And, today, it could be a place transformed by loving care into an area of beauty, a beloved place, nurturing to its keepers as well as to its visitors.

As for me, I believe every garden created by nature or by people has intrinsic elements of the sacred in it. These elements have been recognized as symbolic: the myths of the Garden of Eden or Shambhala, and as divine, such as the ancient oak groves of the Druids as places of worship. Also, cathedral cloisters or temple gardens offered sanctuaries or places where people could be integrated with the powers of nature. Each garden is sacred insofar as our love and attention have recognized it.

What is a sacred garden? It is a place of beauty and profundity. It is a place that brings a sense of the wild places of the world back into the heart of civilization; a place for the human soul to merge with the spirit of this Earth and renew the purpose of humanity. It is a place where the powerful magic of life itself seeps back into the soul; restoring the body and healing the fractured mind; a place of transformation and the emergence of a new, higher, more inclusive state of consciousness.

– CAROL HORN

Every garden is a gateway to a state of mind. One can feel the urge to create one, to participate in nature's endless cycle of germination, growth, flowering, fruiting, seeding, decaying and regenerating. This urge comes from a blessed place within, a sacred garden of the mind. If the image of this inner garden evokes delight, reverence and a sense of transcendent joy, it confers its magic. If nurturing and caring for the growing plants gives a person the whole attention of fingers and heart, this person may find his or her life transformed.

So it is that gardens are burgeoning everywhere today, in backyards or in courtyards, in converted city dumps, on state properties, in rural and urban settings. It is as if each person and each community is seeking ways to serve and to bring back some measure of reverence for the earth and into his or her own heart. By creating new gardens and preserving existing spaces of natural beauty, people have learned they can restore their bruised spirits and create sanctuaries—havens from the stress and pollution of the modern world.

There is no other door to knowledge than the door nature opens; and there is no truth except the truths we discover in nature.
LUTHER BURBANK

The Earth-Peace Garden

With hand-collected rocks, a Navajo working crew of young volunteers prepares stone walkways in the Earth-Peace Garden in Sedona, Arizona.

Imagine an overgrown field in dry Arizona surrounded by pine woods, cacti and acacia being transformed by a small community of gardeners. This garden is bordered on one side by a dry, deep streambed, and by a steep mountain bank on the other. Visualize a quiet resting place, a pavilion for prayer or contemplation or for simply reveling in the majesty of the red sandstone rock escarpments and higher cliffs and ponderosa pine forests.

Visualize the work these gardeners undertook to encourage this six-acre wildness into a garden of love and quiet beauty—their small sacred garden! First, there was the transplanting of cacti from the potential pavilion site to the mountain bank; then came months of Saturdays when volunteers of all ages

An open-air pavillion graces the center of the Garden. Much time and great care were taken to create beautiful places to walk and rest the eyes.

and my backbone crew of adults, my children and grandchildren, even great-grandchildren, all came to help. Next, they cleared land, spread new soil, raked out stones, carried rocks of all sizes to the mountainside bank. There they created a rock garden with wild blue verbenas, orange globe mallow and stands of cat claw, mesquite and yellow-flowered barberry. Next, they picked each flagstone for the terrace around the pavilion and, for the pathways, laid the concrete in which to place them week by week. After some welcome rain, the old field became a growing space to receive wild purple asters, desert marigolds and white horsenettles; daffodils and purple robe, penstemons and iris smiled on the terrace borders. This beloved space is dedicated to Shirley Caris, founder of the

Sedona Creative Life Center, and also to the 17th Karmapa of Tibet, His Holiness Gyalwang Karmapa Ogyen Trinley Dorje, a twin spiritual soul of the Dalai Lama.

If this little garden in Arizona can become a sanctuary, a place where these red sandstone mesas, piñon and juniper forests and diverse cacti form a quiet retreat for the visiting Karmapa and others, then those gardeners have been blessed to create a microcosm of the sacred garden, the Earth.

A landscape, like a man or a woman, acquires character through time and endurance.
EDWARD ABBEY

Across the seas from Arizona, perhaps Claude Monet's extraordinary garden in Giverny, France, remains one of the world's most beloved and visited areas. Originally created by the painter to provide in nature the color contrasts he wanted to experience and transform on canvas, today it constitutes a gloriously lavish bouquet ranging from fiery scarlets and carmines through tangerines, oranges and lemons to every conceivable shade of blue and purple. With colors arranged in mini-environments, a huge tree trunk of linden is surrounded by white feathery baby's breath, punctuated by crimson tulips. A tamarisk tree with weeping pink branches sets the tone for long alleys of stock, iris and variegated tulips. The water lily pond, whose blue-green and white tones Monet immortalized forever, is now contrapuntal in brilliant azaleas. The varieties of plantings and colors change from season to season, but the fiesta continues from April to November, with a necessary time for mulching in between. The love and awe visitors—and workers—bestow upon Monet's dream is a microcosm of what sacred gardens around the world evoke.

Factors such as design, color, fragrance and sheer magnificence—and, most of all, the quality of care and love—all instill a sense of the sacred in some of the world's better known gardens. For example, in the Zen Gardens of Japan, each boulder or raked area of sand becomes a microcosm of a spiritual state of being.

Throughout the Middle East, in Greece, and across the countries around the Mediterranean Basin, in Islamic gardens and the Moorish Alhambra of Spain, there are inner courtyards with tiled pools. In bordering countries of Africa, the countless shade-cooled oases of the Sahara bring salvation and peace to weary travelers. Scotland's magical west coast gardens—Crarae and Arduaine, the inspiring Inverewe garden, and Findhorn on the wild, windswept northeastern coast—create paradises on formerly dam-

JAPANESE GARDEN

aged land. England, and Cornwall, in particular, offer many other extraordinary examples, such as Trebah, Trelissick, and Trengwainton gardens, and sacred wells such as Sancreed.

For its part, the North American continent has a number of legendary gardens: the Green Gulch Zen Center Gardens in Tassajara; California's lush Huntington Gardens in San Marino; Mendocino Coast Botanical Gardens in Fort Bragg; Seattle and San Francisco's Japanese gardens; exotic Botanical Gardens in St. Louis, Missouri, and Phoenix, Arizona; the lovely, private gardens of Charleston, South Carolina, open to the public from time to time. In Mt. Desert Island, Maine, there is the Asticou Azalea Garden which, each June, ignites with a blaze of fiery reds, crimsons, pinks, purples and whites.

In and around the area of Vancouver and Victoria in British Columbia, Canada, are many superb gardens, including the Dr. Sun Yat Sen Chinese Classical Garden in Queen Elizabeth Park, the University of British Columbia Botanical Garden, the Vandusen Botanical Garden and the famous Butchart Gardens on Vancouver Island.

On Washington's Puget Sound, the exquisite

Scenes from Vancouver gardens, clockwise from left: Springtime in Queen Elizabeth Park; Japanese maples in Vandusen Botanical Garden; pebbled court-yard in Dr. Sun Yat Sen Chinese Classical Garden.

Bloedel Preserve has sprouted on land formerly ravaged by logging and quarrying. As more and more people take on the sacred mission to rehabilitate polluted, gutted, strip-mined or clear-cut lands all over the world, Bloedel represents one of many such resurrections.

In Native American gardens across the United States, meanwhile, nature also provides living sacred gardens: forests, meadows, plains, deserts and mountains. In the dry Southwest, the Hopi and Pueblo people construct terraced gardens along the rocky slopes of their mesas and in broad valleys. Both they and the Navajo have developed ingenious "dry farming" methods, which provide healthful sustenance from corn, squash and beans within the limitations of their severely dry climate. The Hopi maintain orchards of fruit trees using this practice. To them and for many tribes farming is a mind-body experience.

It is not enough to understand the natural world; the point is to defend and preserve it.

EDWARD ABBEY

Our archetypal ancestors' belief in the power of trees and in the spirits living in each flower, leaf and plant, was universal; it wove through everyday life and through their ceremonies. For their part, the Druids met in sacred oak groves; the laurel was the holy tree for Apollo's followers; and the apple was the symbol of everlasting life—or beauty—or knowledge. All life was known to be sacred, and each ancient god-spirit ruled a particular domain of land or sea, river, forest, mountain, air and clouds. Humans are only a tiny part of a luminous universe which we must learn to recognize, love and not destroy.

Pan, the goat-footed symbol of nature, was believed to be a powerful and seductive protector of all wild, courageous and beautiful nature. Back into our lives today, as a transformation of Pan, is the more poignant symbol of Gaia—the ancient mother-goddess of Earth, which many people now believe is the living being of the Earth itself. Pan is said to be alive still, leaping across our public lands, in and out of the orange and purple monoliths of Utah's Zion and Arches national parks, sliding down the cliff-sides of Yosemite. His voice and footprints echo in each translucent tributary canyon off Lake Powell, down through the thundering rapids of the Colorado River.

His legendary spirit spreads across the immensity of the white sands of the world, into each desert unique in vibrant colors of rock, in the strange forms of cacti, in spires of radiant cliffs and swirling dust devils. Pan swims in the vast underwater wilderness gardens of the oceans; he touches the coral kingdoms and weaves among the sea anemones and floating weeds. All the exuberant forests of the planet feel his embrace; the mountains quiver and shake their manes of snow into the turbulence of falling waters. Each leaf and each alga, lichen, moss and mushroom of the wild gardens claims his love. They salute his presence in the growing and praise him with the sun.

These legendary oases of the spirit are worldwide. We celebrate them in our hearts and minds, in our literature, our dreams. They have names that bring into our minds cooling waterfalls, raked by sea waves of sand and wild fragrances: Yosemite, Kyoto, Niagara, Boboli and Versailles . . . Eden!

We need to know that all these manifestations of greening glory still exist, as well as how to protect them. We must acknowledge this beauty in our pores, our bones; we must save it, cherish it, nourish it;

we must recreate it in a million brush strokes, sounds, movements, words and actions.

By recognizing the sacredness of our planet, our sacred garden, we discover the means of awakening the inherent beauty that is part of each of us and of confirming our responsibility to preserve and co-create with it.

I am always glad to touch the living rock again and dip my hand in high mountain sky.
JOHN MUIR

25

CHAPTER TWO

Personal Awakening to the Sacred

In wildness is the preservation of the world.

- H. D. Thoreau

I believe that my soul must have been aware of the Earth gardens in which it flourished; however else could I, or any of us who have awakened to the magnificence which surrounds us, recognize the sacred nature of our quest? It is rarely taught in our schools or in our religious upbringings, but Eden lives in each of us as a sacred core waiting to be recognized.

Today, I live with my oldest son in a natural garden in the Southwest, an enchanted land my husband and I discovered and explored before he died. Our house sits at the base of thousand-foot sienna pink sandstone cliffs, with white limestone striations that dance in variegated forms against the pulsing light. At the base of these cliffs emerge outcroppings of pink and yellow-white rocks, covered with patches of blue and green lichen, surrounded by prickly pear and banana yucca, juniper, piñon and the varying greens of dozens of varieties of flowering shrubs and plants—all with protective spines. Here is a cliff rose with wild-strawberry-like blossoms of extraordinary fragrance; there, the spiky leaves and tall spires of scarlet bugler, as well as tiny outcroppings of wild, daisy-like cushions and locoweed, that wild purple lupine so poisonous to animals.

My son, J. Antoine Seronde

The untamed garden of this Arizona wilderness provides a terrain alive—still—with enchanting birds and animals: flocks of orange and black-hooded orioles, mountain bluebirds, larks, mockingbirds, canyon wrens, roadrunners, quail with nodding plumes, rust-sided towhees and juncos. Coyotes sing nightly on the ridges near the house and, in the dry season, deer, cottontail and jackrabbits, as well as javelina and foxes, find pools of water in our wash. We also have our quota of rattlers and bull snakes, scorpions and black widows, each essential to nature's balance.

However, the garden most deeply rooted in my life is the garden that my children helped to create—the family vegetable garden in Maine. Over the years it has received untold tons of manure and compost, originally worked into the stony clay earth by a wonderful old man with an old hand plow. Now we have hands, hoes, mattocks and a modern Troy-Built rototiller. For three generations of family—us, our children, and grandchildren—it has become a tradition that has held us together in a strong bond. Since the children were small (some 40-50 years ago), they have helped to weed, plant, pick and eat the long pole-beans and peas, the New Zealand spinach and a variety of lettuce.

I have a passion for arugula; one daughter always includes nasturtiums, and mustards grow wild between the rows. The scents of freshly-mown hay and spruce forests, peonies, wild roses and sea-salt from the nearby bay pervade the woods and meadows. Fog and high-floating gulls, the wild stony beach with seals basking on the low-tide rocks and a family of bald eagles dominating the coastline with their huge spread-wing presences—these are the summer voices of that land.

I find working in a garden, especially weeding, a panacea for almost all ills. Sometimes, disgruntled by some quarrel or stress, I sit down on the earth or on a sweet-smelling garden-edge lawn. I lift handfuls of humus to my face and fill my nostrils with the poignant fragrance. A mindless happiness comes over me as I pull weeds, or transplant, caressing with my fingers each small green shoot, feeling love coming from the earth into my being. It is the most healing action I know.

BLUE SUMMER GARDEN

Perhaps each of us is a garden filled with seeds, roots, potential stems, leaves, flowers—and weeds! Perhaps the seed in us is a soul which has experienced many transitions in reincarnation.

We all search for our roots, where we have come from, who we are. I do know of my own roots, those extraordinary people who were my forebears: parents and grandparents who became sacred to me because of their sustained love and nourishment. This nurturing, and the diverse gardens they created, were inspirations that evoked this book.

In Glen Cove, Long Island, my maternal grandparents had a white garden filled with phlox, bellflowers, stock and candy tuft, absolutely heady with scent but monotonously white. Stone steps descended into grass walkways among the white rectangles; beyond, a great expanse of dark oak forest with huge trees which were filled with crows and calling jays. Clouds of butterflies fluttered in that garden—skippers, huge yellow and blue

There are two lasting bequests we can give our children: One is roots, the other is wings.

HODDING CARTER

29

and black striped swallowtails and monarchs that would sometimes land on my finger.

When I was nine, I spent a summer at my grandparents' house. That summer was filled with the blue haze of light and the mingled scents of boxwood and salt spray from Long Island Sound, newly mown grass and damp oak leaves. The atmosphere shared the same blue haze and delight of Beatrix Potter's stories—her world of gardens filled with animals and birds mingled happily with mine. My world there was populated with butterflies, an army of beetles, a praying mantis and even a gorgeous

Luna moth. It clung to the front-door screen, a fragile and enormous, lime-colored shadow-being.

And those grandparents! What presences! My grandmother—tall, imperious, her white hair piled high around her formidable but homely face—dominated that household as she filled every room with vases of flowers—huge masses of peonies, syringa, phlox and zinnias—whatever was in season—which permeated the air and our lives with fragrance. She spent hours arranging these flowers, and every table had its bouquet. These colored splashes are happily mixed in my mind with the varicolored Venetian glasses for orange juice, the brilliant Persian carpets and especially the bright-blue Chinese rug in my grandfather's library.

My grandfather was a very different kind of person—reserved, and quiet, who inevitably gave in to my grandmother. He adored my younger brother, and the two heads—one white, the other coppery red—would be seen bending over interminable games of cards or backgammon. Once, Grandpa called my brother and me to follow him out from my grandmother's sight. Furtively, he led us to his bedroom closet, where, from a special hiding place, he withdrew three pieces of Blackjack bubble gum, which we all chewed vigorously, bubbling at each other with suppressed giggles as we gave off powerful licorice fumes.

A portrait of my mother hung in my grandmother's room. She was painted in a flat, Japanese manner but with a luminous yellow background, seen more often in contemporary Western art. Her hair flamed orange-gold against it. She held a gold filigreed fan and her face was very pale and serene. There was a great silence, a still radiance in that portrait by Henry Dirth. It echoed my mother's fragrances: earth-mulch, rose petals, pine needles, chiffon handkerchiefs laced with Chanel No. 5. For me, my mother reigned as a kind of goddess. She was both an elegant grande dame and an earthy peasant. I can still see her floating out the front door in a long apricot-colored evening dress, on my father's arm, to yet another dinner.

Those who dwell among the beauties and mysteries of the earth are never alone or weary of life.
RACHEL CARSON

THE ORANGE PRINCESS

my mother
the orange princess
wove

> sunlight of high stars
> her lambs wool touch
> brick dust and twirling chimney pots
> through panes of smiles
> the cobbled alleyway holding
> horsechestnut burrs and coal dust
> on the snow
> late afternoon tea
> with high-pitched friends
> oasis in the downstairs pantry
>> letters
>> colors
>> furs
>> Chanel
>> and moth flakes
> into a green-gold skein cocoon

the monarch flies
five oceans
seeking prayer wheels
to find
her green-gold tree

In a different part of Long Island, East Hampton, there was another sacred garden, this one belonging to my father's parents, both of them portrait painters, muralists and garden artists. It was bathed in blue light and salt sea-smell mixed with the musky green odor of the nearby lake. Formal circles of orange zinnias surrounded a fishpond filled with goldfish and lily pads in front of the house, and waves of orange trumpet-vines climbed the house's stucco walls. Behind, looking down to the lake, was a terrace scented with white and purple-blue petunias in huge pots, placed on low terrace walls. A wide staircase led down to the lake, where swans fed in the murky, midsummer water. In this paradise I ran wild and barefoot over acres of green lawn between hydrangea bushes with huge blue blossoms, swarms of mosquitoes following. I couldn't have been more than three or four, a princess in an enchanted fairy tale.

These artist grandparents were gentle, remote people, whom I remember particularly through color. My grandmother, always swathed in a diaphanous greenish-blue or purplish printed gown, presided over tea and cookies on the petunia terrace. She spent her mornings painting, usually a still life of flowers. Very early in my life, I began to recognize those flower paintings, swirling in light and pastel colors; she too, had seen early works of Monet and Renoir and had absorbed the color scale of the Impressionists. When I was older, I learned she was also an accomplished portraitist.

I married young to a doctor whose deepest love was marine biology and who was an ecologist long before the word became fashionable. If he could have relived his life, it might have been as an explorer of wilderness, of the long rivers in the pristine canvases of Albert Bierstadt or Remington, of the domains of elk and grizzly, the direct enchantments for a naturalist. His real passion was always for live animals—creatures of every species, their customs, foods and living habitats.

Adele Seronde

As a pathologist, he was a born teacher, and spent years educating medical students. He also taught his love for exploration of mountains, woods and wilderness to each of our five children.

The whole world of nature was his garden.

My husband Joe and I

A PRINCE

There is a prince
  moving in the gray
  and shadowed forest of my heart.
In him the wild deer stray
and song of thrush a silver spiral
  of his love.
He treads as noiseless over pine-needles
  as sunlight,
nor will he break the threads
  of spiders
  crossing in the dew.
No twig nor moss displaced,
  he heals my heart
  with browns and fragile greens
  of lichens and wet ferns.
I lie beneath the leaves.
  He waits in patience
  for my rebirth.

My father, Christian A. Herter

My father, like my grandparents and mother, grew up surrounded by flowers and gardens, color and painting, and this ambiance wove through his life. He loved to direct and plan; he oversaw all the planting and harvesting at our farm where we spent every weekend, but because of severe arthritis, he did not help with the physical labor.

One of the most important garden domains of all our lives was a plantation called Cheeha-Combahee, in South Carolina, which my mother's parents had bought during the Great Depression. This land offered us a unique territory of twelve thousand acres supporting huge moss-draped live oaks, wild lowlands covered with various pines and hardwoods, masses of dogwood blossoms in spring, oaks festooned with wisteria and jasmine. Our low-slung ranch house stood on a point overlooking miles of yellow-grassed marshlands in between two winding silver rivers, the Cheeha and the Combahee, from which the plantation took its name.

This plantation was my father's ideal place for his experimental planning. He had ambitious visions for what could be made of this land economically: pine trees for lumber, oak forests rattling with acorns for pigs, converted marshlands in one area for cattle and other marshlands for rice. He spent time working with the University of South Carolina on an experimental idea to turn the rich delta land, divided by brackish-water estuaries, into feeding ground. First, one needed to dynamite ditches to carry off the saltwater; then, with a huge backhoe on tractor treads, turn over the alluvial soil until it was ready for planting sturdy grasses; then, pasture sun-resistant Brahma cattle on the land.

On paper it sounded marvelous and precedent-setting. But nature did not cooperate. Hurricanes came and flooded the dikes and levees that had been built to support the drainage ditches; screw-worms came and bred in the eyes of the cattle and pigs. A hurricane flattened a large percentage of the standing timber. The rice crop had its own desolate history. We bought an oversized picking and threshing machine to replace

*Everything changes,
and nothing is
more vulnerable
than the beautiful.*

EDWARD ABBEY

the expensive workers who had previously harvested the rice. But that year the rains were so extensive that the rice grew to sequoia-like proportions and that machine sank helplessly into the mud.

Perhaps all these disasters were a heaven-sent retribution for our man-made tampering with nature's basic design. We know now that all those marshes serve special purposes: for holding the silts and rich bottom lands that were being swept to the sea by the rivers and rains; for providing refuge to enormous varieties of migrating birds, as well as a home for crustaceans and shellfish, crabs, shrimp and oysters, and for myriads of insects. In those days we took for granted the bounty of ocean marshlands; today—after developers and sewage plants, garbage fills and malls have invaded these swamps—we are only beginning to recognize our worldwide losses.

FATHER

Tall man, tall elm leaning
into a high sky,
bent with disease and dying
but still with arms outstretched
he stood
at the roadside of the whole world.

Ideas grew tall then too,
living in groves, touching limbs
and exchanging leaves.
Most have been cut down since,
and no Druids guard
our seers.

He stayed rooted believing
that men could change men
through gardening of self;
he touched others with green,
sought substance of water
and soil of each person's worth
to bring fruit.

Elms, like chestnuts,
are passing,
and nobody knows
what they meant to our growing
or language,
the girth of the timber
or how – in the heat of ungrateful worlds'
turning –
they gave shade.

Attracted by my father's professional life,[1] a diverse group of people visited the Cheeha-Combahee plantation over the years—statesmen, diplomats, politicians, writers, artists, lawyers—all drawn together ostensibly for a week of shooting—but, in reality, for a week of communication, of refuge from a distraught world. My mother, as their hostess, was the very spirit of the blue haze and light, filtering

---

[1] See Appendix: Biography of my father, Christian A. Herter, p. 186.

THE FAR
MARSHES
AND SPANISH
MOSS

through the Spanish moss, the breadth and sweep of those far marshes and distant blue islands. She was one of the central loves of my life, and a grounding for my soul.

Father had a dedication to forming, through just treaties and laws, a more compassionate world willing to share its knowledge and its wealth. After years of traveling, of meeting with both domestic and foreign leaders to help solve problems of enough foods and fuels to live by, he taught us that, if we had ideas, we must take responsibility for implementing them. Public service was part of that responsibility.

Both my mother and my father contributed their passion and commitment to all of us, their children.

To know oneself, one should assert oneself.
ALBERT CAMUS

CHAPTER THREE

The Need for Gardens Made Sacred by Love

I'm going to leave a heart in the earth so that it may grow
and flower and adore everything green.

- Rosario Murillo

All of these gardens in my life are sacred to me through the love I have received from them. I have invested all my working energy to share this love with the world around me.

My early world was centered in Boston, Massachusetts. There, many years later, I recognized that there are gardens everywhere needing to be loved, to become sacred to their users. For instance, many of the landscaped grounds around former state hospitals for the mentally ill have been turned into community gardens: small parcels brimming with sunflowers, vegetables and marigolds. Elsewhere in the U.S., abandoned lands have been transformed into sanctuaries where people suffering from illness and substance abuse can work in the earth, becoming part of a living garden that offers the path back to health.

Gated garden walkway

And how is this to be accomplished? At home, many have started to heal souls by taking time to nurture even one beautiful plant on a windowsill, or scooping a small hole in the earth for a seedling or tree. Listening to, and really looking at, that seedling, flower or tree, touching it, smelling its fragrance. These can be direct ways of absorbing its beauty into our being. This can start the process of personal healing. Our attention to that plant is a prayer from the heart, an opening of ourselves to love and compassion, to caring, "our hearts with pleasure fill," as Wordsworth put it. It is a step toward changing our attitudes.

For decades, even for centuries, gardens created sanctuaries in denaturalized, dehumanized urban communities as well as in intimate flowering oases at convalescent homes, hospitals or nursery schools. Gardens, no matter how small, offer protection and food for the spirit as small sanctuaries, as vest-pocket parks; as courtyards in schools, private homes or business complexes; as wayside gardens with seats for travelers or as garden "tot-lots" for little children and their mothers.

In particular, our cities especially need intimate, protected retreats made beautiful by plantings and water and works of art. The Museum of Modern Art in New York City once hosted a Japanese house on a quarter-acre of its sculpture garden as a temporary exhibit. The house, with its garden, was surrounded by a high wall covered with vines. Water, diverted into a stream, flowed beside the sliding doors of the living room. Opposite, about ten feet away, was a high landscaped wall. One day I found myself there in its tiny world of trellised vines, flowers, clumps of bamboo, with fern and iris bordering the stream. No one among the visitors spoke. Sitting by the stream, we watched the clouds and the tops of the skyscrapers and, for a blessed few minutes of utter relaxation, we escaped the city's noise and haste. What a delightful anomaly it was to see New Yorkers with beatific expressions on their faces!

Not just in museums do gardens serve as buffers; they can envelop us in a visual harmony of silence. As the plant kingdom formed a tapestry of green, of music and mirage for our ancestors, so do gardens weave strands of green poetry throughout our lives. At the very least, they can provide screens between us and the harshness and noise of modern life; at the most, they are a real antidote to everyday stress, to despair. Indeed, certain portions of parks or specially designated rooms in schools or convention hotels are increasingly active as demarcation zones for urban dwellers, offering momentary escape and serenity. Such an oasis in an otherwise alien world is Paley Park in Manhattan, with its waterfall drowning out the sound of sirens and the sharp reports of horns and squealing brakes.

My own oasis as a child, on the family farm in Massachusetts, was a tiny clearing in the clay pit swamps, which I reached via homemade causeways of long branches stretching from grass hummock to hummock above swampy water. From my hideaway I could sit with my back against a pine and survey the expanses of marsh: the bulrushes and cattails, swamp maples and the swimming pairs of ducks and the occasional Canada geese. Most of my time there was spent simply daydreaming, breathing in the scent of the pine needles and that marsh-wet earth beneath, somehow healing the hurts of school.

Many years later I was hospitalized twice in Concord, Massachusetts. The first time I was struck by how extraordinarily quiet my room was, protected from the busy highway by a double row of huge white pines, nearly as secluded as my childhood oasis. The second time, two years later, every car was audible and every screech of tires or honking horn; the pine trees had all been cut down to enlarge the parking lot. The resultant noise was a physically disturbing incessant static, which must have subliminally

*For the moon,
the rocks, the land,
our hope—these,
I feel, shall endure.*
WILLIAM DAVIS

affected each patient and member of the staff.

A few years ago, I went to the Addison Gallery in Andover, Massachusetts, where its director, Bart Hayes, had mounted an exhibition that isolated the senses of sight, sound and touch, each to be experienced at a separate time. I participated in the exhibit pertaining to sound, traveling first through a wind tunnel into a darkened two-room space. Surrounding us were noisy examples of everyday static—roars of jet airplanes, intermittent traffic droning and the occasional wail of a far train. In both rooms, speakers emitted individual sounds: waves crashing on a beach, a gunshot, automobile whines, horses' hooves, pounding.

The sedge is wither'd from the lake, And no birds sing.
JOHN KEATS

For a few moments, while listening to a speaker, I was totally immersed in a world of memory and surprised at the shock each individual sound evoked. When I heard a bird-song, a particular white-throated sparrow, I burst into tears. The vision of Mt. Washington's forests and high alpine meadows where white-throats—almost never heard now—call to each other and the thought of the whole lost world of vanishing species reduced me to an indescribable sadness.

How could I have been so shaken? It was that complete concentration on one isolated phrase of sound; no distractions, no static, no escape! I had to hear. It is what we all need: to hear something we *love* with our entire being—its unique message, its urgent exorcism. As that white-throat was metaphor for a whole lost vision, so too can a garden evoke the reality of a Shangri-La.

From coast to coast, in cities large and small, because of the traffic noise, many people may no longer hear the songs of the lark or the robin; because of the increasing ugliness and attendant smog of our surroundings, we're too distracted to see the sunset, the stars, the moon and the trees. The static, unwanted dissonant sound so deafens us that we do not hear our inner selves.

Nowadays, more and more children express their need for a buffer. Unaware of the experience of physical gardens, they protect their inner gardens with screens of music, i-Pods, or sometimes, drugs. The fact is that, whatever our ages, we all need places of refuge, of sanctuary—an oasis of the soul. Hope, however, is no longer just chimera. In the summer of 2008, record numbers of college students left big cities behind and signed up to work on farms and truck gardens. "Welcome them," a Nebraska farmer told a reporter. "We all hope this trend is more than a political statement. We need the young 'uns. We need more farms. Are times truly changing?"

Long ago in Europe, the monasteries of the Dark Ages acted as havens, refuges and places of escape from the depredations of warring tribes and invasions, as well as places of physical and spiritual nourishment, order and harmony. Here, the passion and philosophy of the early Christian church thrived alongside the classics of Greek and Roman thought and literature, which were stored, absorbed and incorporated into the compost that nourished the growing garden of Western thought. The men and women of the monasteries were gardeners and, also, guardians of human aspirations, preservers of a body of knowledge, illuminations and spiritual doctrine.

If you see no reason for giving thanks, the fault lies in yourself.
TECUMSEH OF THE SHAWNEES

Today's monasteries are the churches, synagogues, mosques, Quaker meeting halls, libraries, colleges and foundations, some of which collect, preserve and expand our knowledge while acting as spiritual sanctuaries in our strife-torn society. The challenge of preserving and enhancing our intellectual and spiritual life has fallen to the all-encompassing Internet; the whole world may benefit. In addition, there are small communities all over the world that function as sanctuaries for thought and spiritual enlightenment.

One such oasis of the spirit was a Benedictine Monastery in Morocco called Toumliline, now a leprosarium but once a deep testament to Christian faith and healing. A friend and I decided to visit there because of an initial, extraordinary meeting with one of its monks, Père Placide. It was he who informed us that the role of the monks at Toumliline was to bridge the

Lacock Abbey entrance in the village of Lacock, Wiltshire, England

widening gap between feudal-thinking elders and their rebellious children. Also, he said there was work to be done to expand the overall economy, such as strengthening their schools with reinforced concrete so that they wouldn't disintegrate when the spring rains arrived. He invited us to take part in the life of his monastery, during which time annual seminars were held about new ideas and methods to improve conditions throughout Africa.

During those two weeks, we visited the local markets, helped teach village children, who rewarded our crayon-and-paper escapades with a concerto played on homemade instruments: ocarinas, combs, pots, pans and whistles!

We journeyed to a *ksar* (town) at the Sahara's edge, saw the children riding Arabian horses in from the desert, and watched the threshing of wheat by teams of two mules and three horses pushing a stone wheel round and round. We met the village chieftain in a special ceremony. He was a Berber dressed in a white *djellaba* and turban, sitting cross-legged on a deep red carpet in a cave-like throne room.

A particular adventure took us by Jeep across a desert of multicolored dunes and the foothills of the Atlas mountains. We were harassed along the way by dust devils that seemed to be reaching a thousand feet in the air, leaving all of us with choking lungs and sweltering in claustrophobic heat.

Suddenly, a low line of serrated palms loomed on the horizon. Was it a mirage? Or was it an oasis? It was no mirage! We swam that evening in a pool of deep green shadows encircled by date and royal palms, intense with the aroma of orange groves. Hearing a medley of strange bird sounds, we were lost in a tide of loving—drowned and reawakened—a delicious and revivifying happening.

When we were finally able to see our monk host, Père Placide, he invited us to tea at the home of a recently married couple, and there we experienced the essential loving consideration of this monk. We had met the young man—who'd recently returned from Paris at the insistence of his parents—to be married to a fourteen-year-old child. He looked pale, harassed and disconsolate. At tea, his new wife presided, her new role defined: to bear his sons and to minister—forever—to her mother-in-law. I do not remember the mother-in-law, only that beautiful child, dressed demurely and constantly offering home-

Those who contemplate the beauty of the earth find resources of strength that will endure as long as life lasts.
RACHEL CARSON

baked baklava, fruit and nuts to us all with a smile of such courage that my heart ached. Her husband sat like a closed shell. But our friend, Père Placide, was like a shadow spine beside her, giving her support to each movement, echoing her smile. Later, I asked him, "What will happen to them?" He said, "This is where the real compassion, the inner garden of the spirit, is needed: to mend his heart for this child, and for his elderly parents living in a different century; to help them all accept the deep strength and caring under the frustration and to help this love *live!*"

While I was at the monastery, I had a strange vision during a fever. I had made an appointment to see the Père Prieur, its chieftain, a venerable figure admired widely by both monks and the local population. All I remember was launching an impassioned plea to help create a new Toumliline at my family's place in South Carolina. It would be a protected sanctuary where people of all races could meet equally, hear each other, confer and act together on carefully nurtured projects. I saw the plantation as a center for peaceful resolution of conflicts. I was even certain, in my delirium, that my family would be delighted by the idea!

After my mother died, many friends and family members contributed to create a memorial public garden in her honor. It was situated in a quiet area next to a moat, owned at that time by the Metropolitan District Commission, a state agency in care of park lands and reservoirs, in Christian A. Herter Park in Boston. It was there that the strange dream in Morocco finally came into fruition: a sanctuary for city people, a potential place for discussions, concerts and poetry readings. A group of family and friends have cared for it ever since. In particular, a local resident, Lois Sullivan, who had worked for years with whatever help she could get—her own and foster children and immigrants—to prune, weed, haul debris from the moat, replant and mulch this garden.

Lois Sullivan

In fact, Lois was a foster mother to many lost children and to the helpless and needy in the city of Boston. She had cooked weekly meals at her church for the hungry, attracting students from nearby colleges to help. There was always a bed in her house for weary travelers and a place in her heart for the desperate.

Her advice was sought by people of every age. To me she was a beloved friend. Our friendship was

Nature never did betray the heart that loved her.
WORDSWORTH

forged when the mayor's office asked for help to welcome and feed a policemen's group from Alabama (during the difficult civil rights era of the early 1970s), that was sponsoring an integrated baseball team of teenagers visiting around the country. No one in the city offered to support them. Lois heard of my predicament—our staff had left for the weekend—and she came right over. Together, we mustered enough food and briquettes on which to cook. We spent a wonderful evening with this courageous, anomalous group. And, for the next few years, we worked together at the Herter Center, mostly cooking or gardening with inner city groups and visiting local leaders.

Lois showed me the inner workings and heart of her city and shared a sense of her sensibilities, where bitterness had been replaced by reaching out to the potential in all of us. Sometimes it was a thankless job, but she kept the vision alive, for us as well as for dozens of neighborhood people, who found in the heart of the city an oasis of peace—and amazing gardens. They could gaze at water lilies and huge orange carp in the nearby moat. This moat afforded a waterway where wild ducks raised their families and migrating flocks of blackbirds, towhees,

SHEBA

All in one motion
    you are
        the riding sun of hands
        the earth
        white wisdom of the moon.

You have borne
    the great Black King of the Star
    who followed the new Word
        and knelt.

You have strong hands
    to lift ever so many pieces
        of driftwood
        into quiet arms
        out of the curving
        wind.

It is the Coming.

cardinals, wrens and thrushes filled the clumps of white birches at the water's edge, ringed with scarlet oaks and dogwoods. Lois died in 2000. Waterway waves still reflect her smile.

Ultimately, a single garden, a geranium in a flowerpot or a seedling may not be able to heal. But it will set the tone and help create the atmosphere that allows love to come back. By listening to the voices of the garden, or of the individual flower, one can hear the Spirit, or by whatever name, the Creator. Feeling the plant's living essence, one can feel the pure joy of existence and the beauty of that one beloved plant which changes the world.

BLUE PHLOX AND
WILD CHERRY

CHAPTER FOUR

The Metaphysics of Sacred Gardens

The temple bell stops but I still hear the sound coming out of the flowers.

- Basho, 1690

Evocative teachers, gurus and holy persons are among us to help tap into our inner hearing, to communicate the meanings and translate the languages of animals, birds, dolphins, and other living creatures. Such remarkable seers are guiding us to hear and understand the devic songs of the plant world and what we can learn from them. I, too, passionately love trees, grasses, birds, and animals—and even stones. All along I've thought that it was the artist in me that caused me to memorize their shapes; I always have felt these presences and transformed them into art.

Down through history, there have been storybook tales of mythical creatures: leprechauns, trolls, elves, fairies and wizards, usually associated with nature, specifically with mountains, trees, mushrooms or meadows. Some of these fairy tale creatures did extraordinary feats of goodness; others created evil. They form a strong part of our inheritance of folklore and superstition. By modern scientific standards, however, they are unprovable entities. Yet, for centuries children around the world thought they had seen or played with such beings, and these beings have remained archetypes in our imagination and literature.

Speaking of mysteries, thus far it has not been possible to prove that the Earth has centers of energy connected by what some people call ley lines, yet dowsers have found them. Eastern Indians and Chinese believe them to be sacred sites, and the ley lines to be comparable to human flows of energy which are called body meridians and to energy centers called chakras. Chakras serve as energy modulators within our bodies and are loosely associated with the endocrine system. Chinese physicians and acupuncturists worldwide use their knowledge of these energy flows and corresponding pressure points in their methods of healing.

The Chinese have a term for the balancing of elements in the Earth. It is called feng shui—literally, wind and water. The five elements—wood, earth, fire, water and metal—plus natural and symbolic forms, must be in proper relation to each other in a given landscape.

This ancient Chinese science defines principles to achieve maximum harmony with the natural order. It is a complex process that interprets a language articulated by both man-made and natural forms within the continual workings of the universe. This includes the principles of duality called yin and yang and the five elements, which, in turn, are carried throughout the world by wind and water, moon phases and star alignments, all in recognition of a cosmic spirit, a life force or energy called chi.

A feng shui master reportedly wrote:

Feng shui compass

If a geomancer can recognize Chi, that is all there is to Feng Shui. Chi is the vital force that breathes life into animals and vegetation, inflates the earth to form mountains, and carries water through the earth's ducts. Chi is a life essence, a motivating force. It animates all things. Chi determines the height of mountains, the quality of blooms, and the extent of potential fulfillment. Without Chi, trees will not blossom, rivers will not flow, and man will not be. And while all things—hills, streams, trees, humans, stones—inhale Chi, they also exhale it, thus affecting each other.

According to this tradition, when a person wishes to construct a building, he or she asks a feng shui practitioner to determine not only the most harmonious position on the land, but also to examine the size, shape and even the color of a building. Also to be determined are the direction and turns of overpasses and roads and the angle of a building's corner. Finding such a balance establishes a proper foundation for everything that comes afterwards.

For years, it has been rumored that Western corporations, ignoring this tradition, have arbitrarily built at random in China and the Orient and reportedly later found that nothing went right. Businesses failed. When the British first took possession of Hong Kong Island, they encountered problems in its development, reportedly because they damaged the feng shui in leveling hills, filling in lakes and building roads. The Chinese claimed these difficulties arose because the British had maimed the land's "guardian dragon." The British had begun building the first commercial trading center in a depressed area a mile away from the sea. The resultant low land became swampland and a breeding ground for mosquitoes that carried malaria. When the people began dying, the Chinese workers boycotted the development as "bad feng shui." The British were forced to relocate the center more auspiciously to a site where it still thrives today.

In the U.S. there's a well acknowledged tradition of dowsing to find water, but using this technique for power centers or ley lines is not widely honored. These forces are not measurable by contemporary instruments and, until very recently, were not subject to serious scientific investigation.

Look deep into nature, and then you will understand everything better.
ALBERT EINSTEIN

*Mont Saint Michel in
Normandy, France*

Not so in England, where several grassroots organizations have begun to attract scientifically trained researchers to explore these time-honored traditions.

Furthermore, isn't it fascinating to know that many of the temples, churches, mosques and stupas of the world are built over ancient places of worship, which, in turn, were erected upon places of power selected by dowsers or shamans? For example, the great cathedrals of Europe are located on energy centers containing confluences of deep aquifers and ley lines.

By some means of perception (dowsing, geomancy or perhaps clairvoyance), ancient shamans identified sacred places of great power—sites propitious to the gods.

The stone circles of the British Isles—such as Stonehenge, Avebury, Boscawen Un and the Merry Maidens in southern and western England; the Standing Stones of Callanish, Temple Wood, the Ring of Brodgar on the islands and highlands of Scotland; Newgrange in Ireland; and Carnac in Brittany—are well-known megalithic sites. The famous English cathedral at Glastonbury and the ruins of St. Michael's atop the Glastonbury Tor, as well as St. Michael's Mount in Cornwall, are examples of many ancient sites that have become modern Christian places of power and worship.

It is believed that a major ley line connects more than fifteen sacred sites runs entirely across England, from its eastern coast down its southwestern spine to its farthest tip, and includes Avebury, Glastonbury, Boscowen Un and St. Michael's Mount. A second line is said to connect Salisbury, Old Sarum and Stonehenge; and a third runs between Glastonbury and Stonehenge. More recently, a line has been recognized that runs all the way from Skellig Michael on the southwestern tip of Ireland, through St. Michael's Mount in Cornwall, across to Europe through Mont Saint Michel, Bourges, Lyons and Sacra di San Michele in France. Then the ley line runs through Pisa and beside Assisi in Italy, on across Greece, crossing both Delphi and Athens, the islands of Delos and Rhodes, and finally to Mount Carmel in Israel.

Devas and Nature Spirits

A fascinating and provocative book, *Behaving As If the God in All Life Mattered,* by Michelle Small Wright, affirms what many people have experienced in the famous Findhorn gardens in Scotland: there are nature spirits watching over the welfare and growth of every living creature. Some call them devas, after the Sanskrit word which means shining one or body of light. Each plant has a guardian spirit, or deva, and when we humans learn to work cooperatively with these plant devas, the plant itself flourishes in an extraordinary way. Wright also believes there are nature spirits that guard entire areas.

When these are invaded by humans (cutting down forests, burning, bulldozing, spraying pesticide), the spirits leave, taking away the heart of these areas. Mass produced vegetables no longer seem to have the richness, nutritional content and unique taste that gardeners experience when they grow their own. Have they been sterilized by our actions? Over-designed suburban landscaping serves to impress the neighbors, not to heal the soul.

Findhorn Garden in northern Scotland is an extraordinary example of an amazing interaction between the spiritual energy of human beings and the plant kingdom. It began as a simple gardening venture between a family and a few friends living in a caravan park on the cold windswept sand of a seaside peninsula. It turned into an experiment now known worldwide, defying rational explanation.

Expect your every need to be met. Expect the answer to every problem, expect abundance on every level.
EILEEN CADDY
FINDHORN FOUNDER

The process involved a day-to-day discovery: the collecting of manure, seaweed and grasses by hand to make compost for soil; the planting of each seedling with great love, caring for root, stem and flower. Each received full attention; each yielded new discoveries. Sun, wind, rain and earth were appreciated and praised, as was each growing part of every plant and the spirits of both plants and gardeners. Each deva was conversed with and listened to. The results were phenomenal. Plants, vegetables, trees, flowers and fruits grew to sizes two and three times normal, with such exuberant vitality that observers could not believe their eyes. Findhorn has become a symbol for people around the globe who wish to create a form of community that seeks to learn the language of plants and to know how to transfer this care and love to other people and to live according to the principles of the devas. This magnificent cooperation among gardeners, plants and spirits attracts visitors and visionary gardeners from all over the world.

Clair Reininger, a spiritual landscape architect, had a very real relationship with the devas in her gardens. Her home was cantilevered over a mountain edge on one of the foothills of the Rockies in Santa Fe, New Mexico. Her garden was an exuberant exchange of colors and textures: flowering masses, shrubs, fruit trees and bonsai pines. Her driveway spiraled down from the crest of the mountain to her house. One day, after a violent summer thunderstorm, a ten-foot-high flash flood rushed down the driveway. My friend, horrified, envisioned her entire house and garden hurtling over the cliffs with the water. She shouted, "Devas! For God's sake, hear me now! If you are really there, DO SOMETHING!"

Just then, the torrent rounded the last bend! The roadway, barely ten feet short of her house, suddenly ruptured and a giant fissure appeared, diverting that entire towering wall of water, bypassing her house and rushing down the mountainside!

As Erma Pounds, an American Buddhist lama, recently said, "I believe that the next great avatar of the Earth, the next great leader who will move all men's hearts, will be a naturalist, an environmentalist. He or she will be able to share and teach about the knowledge of all living creatures."

Hopefully, this person will help us to protect and restore the Earth's creatures, to re-create the habitats we have damaged, to understand what each ecosystem requires. Perhaps this person can help us hear what each animate and inanimate creature and substance is saying in voices that our souls and minds can comprehend. We already know, because we hear, amplified, through electronic recording, the songs of dolphins and whales. We also know that animals and birds communicate with each other in ultrasonic sound ranges. Saint Francis must have listened and heard. Legend tells us that living creatures came to his hand.

And we also know that certain ultrasensitive people throughout history have been able to talk with animals and birds, as well as with plants. My friend Erma tells a wonderful story about the late 16th Karmapa, the Tibetan spiritual leader who was considered a twin soul to the Dalai Lama. When the Karmapa came to America in 1974, he traveled everywhere with a retinue of close

Painting by 13th century Italian artist Giovanni Cimabue of St. Francis of Assisi, known as the patron saint of animals and the environment.

followers and a huge cage of birds. When leaving Arizona, the Karmapa and entourage arrived at the airport in Phoenix, in ample time to wait for the plane, so he decided to give the birds a little exercise. Allowed out of the cage, they soared around the vast airport waiting room. Then the Karmapa decided that there was also time to bless everyone in the airport. His helpers were aghast—the plane was due to depart in fifteen minutes. "Oh no," he said, "they won't be ready for another hour. There's still plenty of time." Just then, the loudspeakers verified the Karmapa's words by saying that his flight would be delayed because of mechanical problems.

Then, the Karmapa began blessing his fascinated fellow passengers. Soon the proprietors of all the airport booths and stalls left their businesses, like so many iron filings, lining up to this magnet for their blessings. One waitress, when asked why in her haste she had simply abandoned a tray in front of her bewildered customer, replied, "I don't know, but I know one thing: I want that man over there to touch me." Just after he had finished blessing all the waiting people, it was announced that the plane was ready for boarding. Since the birds were still flying around, the flight attendants panicked. The Karmapa smiled, clapped his hands, and the birds immediately flew back into the cage. Then he made a sweeping gesture over the cage with his arm and they fell asleep, and they all boarded the plane.

There is a legend from a pre-Vedic history in India, that the shamans of the ancient people had a special relationship to and language with the trees, called "senzar," or emanation of consciousness. This "senzar" was directed toward and implanted into the trees—with the air of the sun. As the trees grew, the shaman would take a very thin, fragile, and pliable substance shaped into a disk and press it against the bark of certain trees—presumably from every species. These people had developed a way to convert the energy of the bark pattern into the energy of sound, so it could be broadcast, giving an understanding of the particular history of each tree. The legend continues by saying that these "tree history disks" were coated with gold and hidden in special places, to be found at future appropriate times.

- From the Tibetan "The Book of Dzyan"[1]

Such an appropriate time may come within our own lifetimes. Surely, we will need all kinds of clues, as well as people capable of interpreting these clues, to know how to regenerate life forces and to restore the habitats we are destroying. It will take naturalist teachers of extraordinary patience who will be able to decipher the intertwined patterns of life, to decipher the ecological infrastructures of

decimated areas—the Easter Islands of the Earth. Such leaders, such interpreters, must be filled with not only the scientific knowledge of tree forms, but with compassion and sensitivity to hear their language, to find the hidden disks. Perhaps the unique feminine energy of Tara, Tibetan goddess of spiritual transformation often associated with trees, will nurture, offer compassion and come into full realization in our age.

So many voices to be heard. Perhaps now we will listen!

---

[1] The Book of Dzyan is a reputedly ancient Tibetan text written in the sacred language of Senzar which Helena Blavatzky, the founder of Theosophy, claimed to have seen while studying esoteric lore in Tibet. Its extremely ancient origins remain controversial. Madam Blavatsky claimed it was among other ancient manuscripts safeguarded by initiates and made it the basis for her major work, *The Secret Doctrine*; it was later incorporated into the work of Alice Bailey.

CHAPTER FIVE

The Chalice Well Garden

The highest happiness of man . . . is to have probed what is knowable
and to quietly revere what is unknowable.

- Goethe

A group I traveled with to England was interested in metaphysics. Some were psychics and others were dowsers. Before long I discovered that many shared a common purpose: to restore love to the deep aquifers and ley lines that had been desecrated by bulldozers, by over-development of the land and by polluting the waters.

The year before, my husband and I had spent six weeks in Italy and France, which prepared me for the trip to England. For him, it was a long-awaited reawakening of joyful memories. For me, it was a quest for awakening. I longed to visit places of spiritual intensity, to be aroused by pure pleasure again, to be overwhelmed by inner music. One such moment of intense happiness, back then, came in Florence, Italy, when we were startled awake by the Campanile bells thundering above us from Giotto's famous tower, encircled by wildly careening swallows. We could hear each bell separately, calling with its own voice and vision. Together, they had a deep-throated resonance with the same timbre as whale songs, singing of the magnificence and despair in the world.

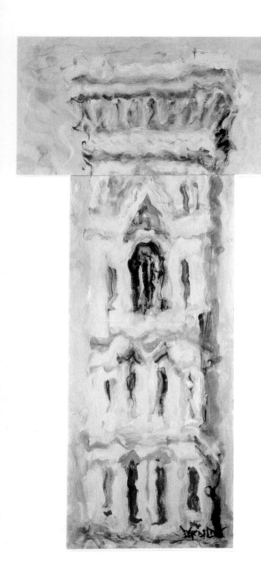

GIOTTO'S CAMPANILE
My painting depicts four of the five levels of the campanile.

Another moment of recognition occurred in Arezza, Italy. On a rainy Sunday morning I wandered into a dark church; the congregation was just leaving and the organist was still playing. The only light shone upon the altarpiece, an eight-paneled pyramid created by one of the famed Lorenzettis. The colors were luminous; the golds, scarlets and blues were burning in quiet flame. Riveted, I sat for an hour, immersed in the poetry of that painting. As I floated in a blaze of inner radiance, the Bach arias intensified each second.

Still another illuminating experience happened in France, where St. Austremoine, a Romanesque cathedral in Issoire, had just been restored. Although I remembered it from 20 years before as being unique, I was unprepared for the vision: a place of the spirit flaming in gold light, vibrating in fire. Columns of sienna-rust-red rose high into Corinthian swirls of moss green. Arches in between were resplendent in scarlets and golds; the altar was surmounted by the old, newly cleaned, sculptures from the 11th century. On the sienna columns was a repeated pattern of diagonal V-shapes enclosing intertwined circles.

These felt symbolic, but I did not know their name or purpose. Had they a meaning I had known or forgotten? Their mystery stayed unresolved within me, and I felt that my spiritual search in Europe was incomplete. However, during my journey to southwest England the next year, I resolved that mystery. It happened on that trip which ranged from sites of power in Cornwall, Dorset and Devon, to the standing stones of Avebury and Stonehenge in Wiltshire, and to Glastonbury in Somerset.

Glastonbury is the town of the Arthurian legends, the compelling stories of the Knights of the Round Table and the Holy Grail. Here was the home of Merlin, of Avalon, of the High Mound called the Tor, surrounded by the twelve signs of the zodiac, which can be seen from airplanes.

It was when we visited Glastonbury that I saw the waterfall basin in the Chalice Well Garden, and the shape of those intertwined circles [1] of the Issoire Cathedral came back to me. I recognized that here lay my truth, the answer to my spiritual search. This symbol, I learned, was called the Vesica Pisces. It is considered part of sacred geometry, which incorporates the three sacred roots (v^2, v^3, v^5) that may be as old as eternity. Certainly, it means, within the Christian community, the intersection or joining together of the eternal and temporal. In this overlap lies the Pisces or fish, the sign of Jesus Christ in the Church.

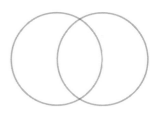

Vesica Pisces

Here, then, as early legend has it, Christ himself, brought by Joseph of Arimathea to study the wisdom of the Druids, must have come to this ancient site. It is said that he blessed the well-head, which is now called the Chalice Well. The lid which covers it is in the form of the Vesica Pisces.

Another legend has it that, after Christ's death, Joseph of Arimathea came back bearing with him two flagons: one of Christ's blood and one of water from his wounds. Joseph claimed that when he poured the blood as a blessing into the spring, the waters created a second stream, which turned red. Perhaps these flagons correspond in symbol to the red and white waters of the two springs that now join at the Chalice Well and flow downstream through the Chalice Garden as waters of healing. To this day, people from all over the world come to this garden to be reaffirmed and redeemed.

After entering the garden and seeing the water flowing into a basin formed into the shape of the Vesica Pisces, one is drawn gradually to the well itself. And there, by the Chalice Well, covered by a lid with the same sacred design, the Earth was actually trembling (probably from the rush of the subterranean waters). I, too, began to tremble and, for no describable reason, to weep.

It was as if all the anguish of the Earth reached up with the sorrow of a land whose spirits had fled, as if the weeping of the whole Earth entered my bones, and the tears were part of Christ. I sat on a nearby bench as alone in that somber, poignant garden as if I had been in Gethsemane. And, in the falling of my tears was a soul-cleansing energy, a catharsis—a purifying—as in part of a Navajo prayer

---

[1] The shapes on the Issoire Cathedral columns were not exact vesica pisces, but were similar and, to me, symbolic.

chant: "With a place of great sorrow in me, I wander. In beauty, I wander."

I was gradually overcome by a feeling of affirmation—an affirmation of my love for the land and the sky and the sea and all their creatures; of my creation of gardens wherever I have lived; of the continuity of the love for the Earth in my family, generations past, present and future. But more than that, it was a declaration of principle. This was to be my mission: to encourage creation of new gardens of hope and healing, spiritual gardens anywhere and everywhere, and to find kindred souls fired by the same mission.

What might this Garden of the Chalice mean to all of us today? A symbol, a challenge, a precedent, a goal, a sanctuary? All of these? What if we were to bring back love into the dark and wasted places of the Earth, into the aquifers of our soul and of our minds, through co-creating Gardens of the Chalice throughout our Earth? What if small groups of us all over the world worked together with the living creatures, with Gaia herself?

What if we pooled our human resources—mental, spiritual, physical and material—and gave of our labor to create small oases of beauty to be loved and maintained? These could be gardens of healing dedicated to all those who

Loving one another, we take the sting from death. Loving our mysterious blue planet, we resolve riddles and dissolve all enigmas to contingent bliss.

EDWARD ABBEY

Chalice Well, Glastonbury, England

suffer, to those who face challenges and also to our children. Together, we could bring soul-nourishment into the Earth and the aquifers of our being and, in so doing, become healed.

YELLOW FLOWER BLANKET IN MAPLE GROVE

We abuse land because we regard it as a commodity belonging to us. When we see land as a community to which we belong, we may begin to use it and love it with respect.

ALDO LEOPOLD

Healing of Community

CHAPTER SIX

Urban Gardens and Playgrounds

*What an extraordinary time to be alive. We're the first people on our planet
to have real choice: we can continue killing each other, wiping out other species,
spoiling our nest. Yet on every continent a revolution in human dignity is emerging.
It is re-knitting community and our ties to the earth. So we do have a choice.
We can choose death; or we can choose life.*

- Frances Moore Lappe

In the wake of earlier riots, and after Martin Luther King's murder, entire sections of cities burnt down. Shells of houses remained, along with abandoned rubbish, weed-filled lots and lost people. It was the widows, grandmothers, handicapped, abandoned children and drunken survivors who inherited these wastelands, the lost city lands. It was they who reclaimed them. With nothing but primitive tools, (spoons, broken shovels, pots for watering and a few seeds), they began to plant survival gardens.

This urban garden movement began to spread from burnt areas to empty dump lots and abandoned land. Gradually, blighted areas became food-producing refuges of greens and flowers. People made fences from trashed wood and wire knit together. And they exchanged seeds, plants and smiles. With gardens burgeoning, these actions have begun to bring communities a sense of pride and sufficiency. However, these gardens needed protection. Developers then took notice: there was newly attractive real-estate to be exploited! Valuable lands to be used for free! Such battles are being fought all over America now, with developers claiming ownership and gardeners protesting and even lying down in front of bulldozers.

In Boston, in the early '70s, help came in the form of an articulate legislator, Mel King. He knew the plight and feelings of the inner city, and he made protection an issue of such clarity that he persuaded the city council to pass a law giving the elderly, the handicapped and the indigenous the right to improve empty city lots by creating gardens.

In one of Boston's most dismal housing projects, tenants organized and decided to make a community garden on a small space of nearby wasteland. They agreed that the work of planting, maintaining and harvesting would be shared by all tenants and that the men and teenagers would protect it. As a result, that summer was a time of relative calm and pleasure. Interest in the garden was paramount. Crime and vandalism remained at a minimum. What started as an experiment in a desperate place became a means of salvation.

In Boston's South End Urban Renewal, there was an attempt to build a major highway through the heart of an old residential area. So many objections arose that the city fathers relented; the opened-up area stood vacant until legislator Mel King designated it an area for neighborhood gardens. Subsequently, it was transformed into a ribbon of greens and rainbow colors of a thousand hearts and hands.

There is another extraordinary example of how citizens took charge of their lives in the face of certain demolition of their area, this time at the hands of the Boston Redevelopment Authority (BRA). This also happened in the South End, in a four-block section inhabited mostly by Puerto Ricans. Upon hearing of the BRA's plans for razing the area, a neighborhood priest sent a Spanish-speaking college student to every house, asking the residents to meet with the Harvard Urban Extension Service (U.E.S.) students to plan alternative community housing to serve them. It took a summer's worth of patience on the part of the U.E.S. students to elicit the residents' ideas and transform them to blueprints.

Perseverance is more prevailing than violence; and many things which cannot be overcome when they are together, yield themselves when taken little by little.

PLUTARCH

70

Urban gardens

PLANTING

greening

the voices called out through the cities
and we called too
"plant with your bones and your marrow
a living tree

cover the brick-ends and shards
with black earth of your blood
and grow forests of corn and sweet melon
in the rich tears

the roots of your patience will welcome
a whole smile
delivered from the green heart of the city
which is now yours"

When the time came to testify before the BRA
(their legal right), the community had another model
to offer as an alternative. An open fairway of grass and
flowers would run through the center of the four blocks,
including an interior island with a central walkway
and seating. All cross streets would be eliminated. The
central island would accompany housing facilities, small business stores, a residence for the elderly, a job
center, a medical clinic, a daycare center and a school. This model was adopted, and this self-sufficient
community continues to thrive today!

Playgrounds as Inner Gardens

Programs that cultivate the inner garden, the garden of the soul, are analogous experiences for both
old and young. Such a program exists in Britain and Denmark and is called an "Adventure Playground."

It provides a focal meeting place for blossoming teenage ambitions and dreams.

This program evolved after the Second World War, when the ground in London remained raw with craters from the bombing. These areas turned out to be ideal playgrounds for young people. They turned debris into makeshift houses with ladders, towers and tunnels.

A number of thinking people observed these youngsters playing for hours. The English landscape architect and promoter of child welfare, Lady Allen of Hurtwood, transformed those observations into structured educational tools. She was able to persuade the Ministries of Education and Labor to allocate sufficient annual funding to train two architect-carpenters to supervise a summer playground with a particular purpose: to act as guides and teachers—only when necessary.

For example, after an acre of flat ground or a rubble-filled dump lot was selected, cleaned and fenced, a mammoth pile of old lumber was dropped in. Then the two guides, laden with hammers, nails, crowbars and planes, invited local teenagers at a certain time of day to transform their own fantasies into reality. The teenagers soon learned, with the help of proper tools and occasional hints about stresses, to build and rebuild! Whole cities rose and fell: towers, perches, labyrinths, halls and swings. Each night gates were closed so no one could enter to vandalize.

At summer's end, the neighborhood children invited everyone to a huge bonfire and cookout. Whole neighborhoods, thankful for this welcome diversion for their children's summer hours, turned up with joy. In fact, in many instances, the Adventure Playground spawned adjoining projects: tot-lots for the babies; seating arrangement for mothers; teahouses, swimming pools and clubhouses for all. One further step led to actual gardens.

Why this idea has not caught on in the U.S. remains a mystery—perhaps young people spend too much of their time in the video arcades shooting down space invaders, or repelling rival gangs. Perhaps it is because many park departments insist on all-concrete playgrounds, where nothing can be moved or taken away. Also, since many playgrounds lie within proximity to elderly people who cannot stand the noise of vivacious children playing, perhaps officials feel that concrete fixtures will create less noise.

We may either smother the divine fire of youth or we may feed it. We may either stand stupidly staring as it sinks into the intermittent blaze of folly, or we may tend it into a lambent flame, with power to make clean and bright our dingy city streets.

JANE ADDAMS

singing! At the end of the day, sweaty, triumphant and wildly happy, we made an impromptu ten-foot barbecue pit out of leftover cement blocks. We gathered remnants of wood, lit them and grilled steaks and hot dogs for everyone. Then, with portable CD players blaring, we danced in the streets!

Leader and organizer for this playground, an outstanding implementor of other Summerthing events, was Drew Hyde, a bouncing dynamo of a small man with enormous energy and buoyant sense of humor. He spent weeks with a volunteer college crew planning and collecting materials for this event.[1]

This excitement filled me with the insight that working together with some neighborhood group to create a needed place, which could be loved and cared for, was what I wanted most in the world. I wanted to help, inspire, convene and participate in re-creating or building new environments where people could realize their inner gardens, own their potential strengths and be empowered.

The main lesson was that playgrounds—inner gardens—should be places of joy, change, challenge and art. Most of all each playground should allow movement and recognition that each age group needs its own kind of challenge: jungle gyms and slides for the toddlers, swings for all ages and adventure playgrounds or equivalents for teenagers.

Obviously, other sports activities do help release and channel some of these energies, but, for the majority, Outward Bound programs offer the best substitutes, each geared specifically to the needs of that community. In his essay *The Moral Equivalent of War* William James visualized opportunities other than war, particularly for the young, to bring out the heroic responses to the horror that war evokes. And, from that essay, so many programs have been spawned.

American "Outward Bound" programs are direct descendants of the schools instituted in Switzerland and Scotland by the German educator, Kurt Hahn, Ph.D. These early programs proscribed periods of intense physical training. This was followed by a testing period in which the participants had to learn to trust each other and support whoever proved, under duress, to be the weakest link in their chain. They then

Play is the sculptor which shapes the life of a child. He confides his dreams to his play and becomes what his play is. We must make the play time of all children and the free time of the rest of us richer, more satisfying, more enobling.

WARREN G, HARDING

---

[1] See Appendix, p. 187.

could accomplish certain dangerous actions requiring great courage, such as rescuing survivors from airplane or skiing accidents on a Swiss mountainside, or saving shipwreck survivors off Scotland's rocky coast.

These training programs were carried out within the normal structure of a basic arts education. In fact, teenagers who took part became so adept in their exciting work in Scotland that they became incorporated into National Coast Guard and Service programs. Prince Charles trained with many youngsters at Gordonstoun in Scotland, a school founded by Hahn that taught firm principles of human conduct and that such service to others is more important than self-service.

Chris Moore, a leader in Boston, devised his own Outward Bound response to his neighborhood of teenagers. Although he had been given an old gymnasium in Dorchester to use for basketball, he felt it wasn't enough. He wanted to open up the field for his charges, so he visited a friend who was the director of the Head ski corporation, who, about to go out of business, gave all his old ski equipment to Chris. This was the beginning of a winter ski program on the mountain slopes of New Hampshire and Maine.

Each year, Chris persuaded and cajoled students into taking summer jobs (often going himself to rouse them out of bed to ensure that they arrived on time at the jobs he had procured and that they were building up self-respect and self-discipline). One summer the Metropolitan District Commission gave him a small parcel of state-owned land near today's Kennedy Center on Columbia Point. There, he and his teenage followers built a wharf. He begged and borrowed materials, and his friends gave him a small group of sailing boats and a teacher. By the end of the summer, their first ocean-going ghetto fleet was launched.

In the next two years, he and his children sailed all over Massachusetts Bay, picnicked on the Harbor Islands and made contact with the Outward Bound group there. He said, "My aim is to build enough confidence in these kids so that by summer they are not only holding jobs, or learning to become radio men or mechanics, but are working together with the Outward Bound kids. Then I know they'll be able to cope with anything." By summer's end these children had developed a strong sense of responsibility. Their inner gardens were blooming.

This country will not be a good place for any of us to live in unless we make it a good place for all of us to live in.

THEODORE ROOSEVELT

CHAPTER SEVEN

Visionaries and Transformers

Where is a garden of wisdom where lost people can meet,

so deep in the garden-etched fragrance of wind-blown flowers

that we offer our fragmented souls, becoming complete?

Is there a garden of pleasure so replete

with happiness that we make of lost minutes verdant and burgeoning hours?

Where is a garden of wisdom where lost people can meet?

- Excerpt from "Villanelle" by Adele Seronde

To wrestle a garden out of a filthy, rubbish-filled dump is a physical and spiritual challenge. Digging out the rubble, making or transporting the soil, planting, fencing and maintaining, weeding and harvesting—all these can become models of community cooperation and training under real leadership—particularly for young people.

In Germany, World War II left mountains of rubble and devastation. There, people of all ages in the cities shoveled small piles of bombed-out remains to a designated place, making a small mountain.

The late Silvana Cenci

Never doubt that a small, group of thoughtful, committed citizens can change the world. Indeed, it is the only thing that ever has.

MARGARET MEAD

Then, they hand-carried more earth to cover the mountain and planted grass and trees, thus converting ruins into parks and winter playgrounds for sledding. Civic pride was built in the process.

Although some people believe that they need land, proper tools and money to garden, they can start a garden with nothing but a patch of barren ground without good soil or manure and with no money, and only elementary tools. What they do need are two able hands, a strong back, imagination—and friends.

A dear friend, Silvana Cenci, a Florentine sculptor by profession, did just that.[1] She bought an old farm in Maine and transformed a rubbish-filled plot of tired land into a jungle of flowering plants, trees and vegetables. Her Italian ancestry and childhood—a cultural background that includes love and respect for the Earth and a passion for growing things—taught her what a garden could be. This allowed her to know that the transition from nothing to everything is possible. What she accomplished in five years is a small miracle.

Hundreds of new trees now grace formerly bare ground: groves of birches, an avenue of Lombardy poplars, mountain ash, maple and locust, in addition to thousands of wildflowers whose seeds have been spread by the current flock of birds. Woodchucks, squirrels, skunks, chipmunks and rabbits have also welcomed their new habitat. Flower and vegetable gardens feed both humans and wildlife.

* * * * *

[1] Silvana Cenci came from an old Florentine family. She won a scholarship to MIT in one of its first classes accepting foreign students in the early 1950's. She lived on hard work and imagination for years by renovating and then selling old houses. As a sculptor, her aesthetic vision evolved into forming her work in stainless steel with small explosives; she would then weld gold onto parts of the forms to create extraordinary surfaces that could reflect passing colors. Her work almost always embraced the plant forms she loved.

Many varieties of human misery exist, and one of them is the misery of being totally ignored and neglected. In 1968, a few dedicated people in Boston were addressing basic needs and rights. But, after the city exploded in fire and rage over Martin Luther King's murder, state legislator Katherine Kane decided that creative measures were needed to unify the city.

Katherine Kane

Using the model of Cleveland's summer festival of the creative arts (made possible by a communal outpouring of nickels and dimes) Kane urged Boston's mayor and city council to approve a similar initiative. She appealed to the people of Boston to take pride in their city, building on the trust from her earlier efforts with residents on the South End to clean up their neighborhood, repaint doorways and courtyards, remove garbage and plant gardens in empty dump lots.

Her remarkable executive ability, coupled with her courage, inspired a resounding acclaim in all the neighborhood leaders for a city celebration of the arts. "Summerthing" was born. It brought together such diverse groups as the Boston Symphony and Boston Ballet, as well as local jazz, rock and dance groups to every city park and meeting place. Old vehicles, broken-down hearses, milk wagons and flatbed trucks were painted bright yellow and emblazoned with "Summerthing" decorations and its logo. These carried musicians, artists and players to their destinations, as well as local volunteers and college students to help at every level.

A crafts mobile, filled with factory outlet odds and ends and staffed by suburban residents who wanted to participate, was driven to parks and closed-off streets. Their mission was to engage the city's children in creating musical instruments, flags and banners, fanciful objects and toys that could be carried around their neighborhoods in triumphantly noisy parades! (Building on experiences, a crafts mobile leader, Elaine Gurian, later, worked in the Boston Children's Museum!) "Summerthing" was an important diversion. It helped deflect the still rampant fear and hatred within the city. It was not a panacea, as we artists had hoped, but it did calm down and unite the people.

How important was it to have such diversions? They provided interest and joy and deflected the overwhelming fear, the hatred and violence, spawned by M. L. King's murder, until people calmed down. I participated in this festival, in the wake of riots, as co-coordinator of visual arts. My first assignment was to fetch a load of acrylic paints for the mural program. Two Black Panthers joined me. They proceeded to paint a wall as background to a new playground and a basketball court designed by a team of M.I.T. students. Their murals, one depicting a black man hanging (soon changed to a white man), and the other, depicting Stokley Carmichael hurling a Molotov cocktail at a white army, raised the hackles of both communities.

In shock, I reported this outcome to Katherine Kane, who asked, "Well, are these murals of Diego Rivera quality?" When I replied no, she said, "Never mind, there will be others that are! Go ahead with the program!" We did, and there were! Indeed, those two Black Panthers worked with the local teenagers, telling them to respect and protect the murals and their playground, as well as the children using it. So they spent that explosive summer of 1969 painting instead of making trouble.

During that summer, some 68 murals appeared all over the city. In the South End, murals seemed to communicate with each other from building to building—like rams' horn trumpet blasts across the mountains in the Far East—as if they were voices of freedom announcing, "We are people! We want everyone to know this is *our* city! We care about us! Each one of us has something to say!"

For one 125-foot-long by 25-foot-high mural, I designed an outline. Artists from culturally diverse neighborhoods composed the rest of the mural, each having an allotted section. For five days we painted, inspired by each other's work, blending our colors and shapes together. We had voices from all the black, Hispanic, Lebanese, and European ethnic communities, except the Chinese component. We asked a passing Chinese teenager to join us and add her community's message. She painted a simple calligraphic figure on a white background. It meant "mankind"!

The following summer, with a team of ten students, we had an opportunity to create playgrounds, plant gardens and paint more murals. We made environments in which people could change their physical places or spark changes that spurred loud reactions—not always good! One of our playgrounds earned so much envy among teenage denizens of a neighboring area that it was destroyed—we had to

That which we persist in doing becomes easier, not that the task itself has become easier, but that our ability to perform it has improved.

RALPH WALDO EMERSON

take it down and haul the pieces away!
Being young and inexperienced, we
were often inept as well. But we were
brazen enough to accomplish things no
one thought were possible, promoting
residents of community neighborhoods
to say, "Well, we could do that better if
we really planned things properly!"

Between 1968 and 1973, buoyed
each summer by a vibrant wave
of energetic college students, this
program brought joy, excitement and
relief to the city and, in all, uplifted it.

In retrospect, Katherine Kane,
that slightly built, beautiful, agile
woman, with ebullient humor and
energy, nimbly circled around the
usual bureaucratic obstacles of static
decrees and stubborn people and
faced the real dangers of the city's
disintegration. All of us who had the
privilege of working with her realized
that she was sharing with us what we
all needed, how to make changes, in
ourselves.

SUMMERTHING

a festival
        of fireflies
                        flickering across the field
        of an entire city –
                simultaneously
                                everywhere –
ushering in the dusks of summer with trumpets
                                        kettledrums
                                        and flutes
        electric guitars and singing colors on the walls –
distributing an offering –
        a rainbow bridge for folk to mount the stage
                        become the act
                                        and soar –
Summerthing –
        against the bonfires set by a century's
                        accumulated rage
a festival of fireflies
                is brief –
small pinpricks of lumia in the wider night   – still –
                magic
                                in a wizard's hands

CITY'S HEIRESS

You laugh among all the King's men.
Not bending to a vision's weight   but entering it
        Within its full circumference.

                                        You measure

    every detail with your bones
        trying on each crisis for size,
knowing what place the heart must hold
        within the armored shirt,
        what competency shield.
And though your span is always mercurial – leaping
        the rainbow arches between gods and men –
                You are not partial to haloes.
With your helmet of Athena
        you would protect Prometheus –
                that titan bringing
        unheroic fire to nourish the city's poor.
But the King is adamant
and works behind closed gloves.
His red-royal vestments of the sun
        Are torn to fragments
                by non-majesty of minions.
When will the moon be rewoven through your hands
                to form the purple and ermine cape?

APOCALYPSE

84

Another stirring vignette begins with Jack Powers, a poet, who ran a small Boston gallery/meeting place called "Stone Soup." Jack was a towering, black-bearded, blue-eyed Irishman with an afro hairdo of wild, curly black hair. He attracted every female within miles! In this gallery he welcomed artists and performers with whatever entertainment and food they could jointly provide. Jack also worked in a local settlement house, becoming more and more concerned with elderly people who seemed to have very little support or pleasure in their lives; many were homeless and hungry. So Jack started a monthly supper that he cooked himself and served with volunteer help.

The numbers grew from 14 to 20 eager participants and, when a local tenement burned down and its occupants became homeless, he prevailed upon the nearby church to house them. Jack provided weekly meals from whatever donations he could collect. His diners soon became 50 and, in the 20 years following, increased to a weekly 150. Although he no longer cooks one meal a month himself, the increasing evidence of more and more sick and homeless people on the streets has caused him to help other concerned groups.

One day Jack visited a local shelter with a load of donated chairs. There he and a friend looked out the windows and saw a magnificent view—a long slope down to the sea and the cityscape beyond. After years as a major supporter and gardener of the Boston Urban Gardeners, he instantly realized that this area, now covered with brambles and weeds, could be converted into a two-acre garden to help feed the homeless. He shared his dream with a friend, who immediately responded, "Can you do it for $500?" Jack nodded, yes. He had seed money.

How to proceed? By begging for help from the Massachusetts Halfway Houses, Jack garnered a 20-man, pre-release prison work force. His friend, Julie Stone,[2] from Boston Urban Gardens (BUG) came to help him work and supervise. Together, they bought fencing materials (to protect the garden from skunks and woodchucks), and seeds and hoses, too. They borrowed tools and persuaded Project

Despair shows us the limit of our imagination. Imaginations shared create collaboration, collaboration creates community, and community inspires social change.

TERRY TEMPEST WILLIAMS

---

[2] See Appendix, p. 187.

View of the Boston skyline from across the Charles River.

Rebound, a drug rehabilitation program, also located nearby, to lend another 25 young men. With hand tools and posthole diggers, energy and laughter, they converted that forgotten slope into a resplendent garden of sunflowers, nasturtiums, tomatoes, lettuces and marigolds—plants that would grow quickly and provide salads in that first year. The harvesting and final turning of the soil was followed by a major feast—an event most of the homeless people had never dreamed could happen.

As this experiment turned into a yearly event, the rehabilitation center needed its own garden and help to create and supervise it. An ever-increasing number of prison inmates, homeless and addicts, turned from this real pleasure and soul giver, to their own gardens. At the feast Jack provided poetry or music (with donations given by a North Shore poetry association called WAIL). During the last year, some of these people whose lives were so fragmented reportedly became whole again.

While serving as director of the Boston Housing Authority, another tall, charismatic Irishman, Daniel J. Finn, saw and felt the desperate needs of people trapped in public housing projects. Later, as a vice-president of Boston University, he addressed some of these needs. Besides creating many small parks, over a period of 30 years, he initiated some beautification projects, including restoration of beaches, lawns, buildings and apartments for the elderly.

Finn believed that public spaces should be made available, if not by the city or state, at least by churches and universities for the general well-being of people. In his opinion, these small parks should be attractive, not ornate and of low maintenance, so that they have a better chance of surviving, even if funding is difficult to obtain. They should include comfortable street furniture and resting places and water features, such as waterfalls, fountains, gardens and pools, as well as pieces of art designed to make a statement and be easily maintained. The 16 pocket parks Finn created at Boston University, which comprised anywhere from a few hundred square feet to a full acre, included major pieces of sculpture by Boston University graduates.

Daniel J. Finn

In order to attract sculptors, he advertised each park project in the university magazine, asking any artist who wanted to participate to write and send him a design. These designs were reviewed by a jury and, out of some 200 to 300 applicants, 25 were selected. While the university supplied materials for the work, artists were asked to donate the finished art. In return, they received such excellent publicity that many became widely known after their sculptures were installed and their work received acclaim. All funds for these parks were solicited from outside the usual university sources, with the approval and support of the university's then-president, John Silber.

Spread all over the BU campus, these parks became usable space—places where students,

There is always complexity to our actions and there's always uncertainty. The only thing I, or anyone else, can do is to create possibilities that support aliveness.

THE LATE KARL LINN

faculty and visitors could picnic and converse, study or simply lie on the grass. These spaces, which could be emulated in a thousand campuses, create an atmosphere of welcome. They speak of Finn's concern for the nurturing of all the people he worked with who served in ways well beyond the definition of their immediate jobs.

When Karl Linn, another visionary, came to America, he dedicated the passion that he had used for other energetic causes to create some of the first vest-pocket parks in Philadelphia. An extraordinary man, born in Germany and emigrating to Israel, Karl Linn became an activist in the Stern Gang, an organization that protested Britain's dominant role in the resettlement of Jewish people. In America he had a fabulous capacity for inducing help from neighborhood groups, particularly teenagers, who were the urban lost souls most in need of courageous leadership.

In her article "Down-to-Earth Visionary" in *Sierra Magazine,* staff senior writer Marilyn Berlin Snell wrote:

> *The idea of a commons is key to understanding Linn's work. In a 1999 article for* New Village *magazine, he argues that an inherently sacred relationship exists between living creatures and nature. "From time immemorial," writes Linn, "people of indigenous or land-based culture have celebrated their connectedness with nature as an integral part of their daily lives. Free and enduring access to air, water, and land assured their sustenance and survival." According to Linn, urban community gardens are the last remnants of the commons in contemporary life . . . .*
>
> *Karl Linn insisted "that people have the capacity to spontaneously transform their environment with very few means. . . ."*

Linn's urban parks became the models for small retreats, tiny oases of beauty throughout the cities. They include vest-pocket parks with a wall of water here, a few benches around a fountain or next to a stream or pond there, and a desert garden with a river of blue tile where water is unavailable.

ROADSIDE WILD CHICORY

sentinels

    they watch

    with

ragged delft-blue eyes

    the workings

        of the city

    rust-subverted

        train tracks

    questing cats

    in garbage   old women

veined

    with swollen stockings

    lovers   drunkards/denizens

    of unsafe parks

this populace of chicory

    is born to wastelands

rising out of layers

of beer cans

humus   torn plastic

        to survey

the many-colored coats

        of Joseph

being sold by brothers

into developers' arms

even

    when the bull-dozers pass

        they rise

tireless guardians

they do not weep   but stand

    on the vacant lots

multi-faced weeds

    ready to spread

        seeds of survival

CHAPTER EIGHT

Lily Yeh and the Village of Arts & Humanities

Art is not what I do, it is what I am.

- Lily Yeh

Once, several years ago, I visited a surprising oasis in the heart of an urban desert in North Philadelphia. Amidst miles of dilapidated houses, littered streets, graffiti and rubbish, there stood a narrow, three-story house whose modest door announced, "The Village of the Arts and Humanities."[1] The center of this oasis was a three-block cluster of parks, community gardens, educational facilities, art workshops and offices that served thousands of low-income people.

Beyond the village, a large pile of debris, mud and weeds was testimony to what had been there before. Everywhere, workers were transforming the rubble into vegetable and flower gardens, into walls and benches. They were also rehabilitating gutted houses into new habitats, almost Moorish in feeling,

---

[1] See Appendix, p. 188.

some decorated with murals. All were now lived in. Up the street, I could see that the entire exterior of a teaching building was covered by a three-story mural with an outdoor stage at its foot.

This rehabilitated house contained an attractive office and a long rectangular area for teaching the arts, drama, poetry, as well as reading and writing. Children from about six to 12 years of age were discussing and acting out some animal characters, perhaps practicing for one of the many upcoming performances on the outdoor stage.

Behind this building sat a large park with paths, flower gardens and a courtyard area with strange upright figures splendidly tiled in mosaic. In the shade of the building people were playing chess, and others were trundling wheelbarrows. One man was laying mosaic tiles into a design on one of the freshly plastered houses. He was chipping out and forming the first colored shapes for the mural from a great rectangle of colored clay, which had been fired in the village kiln.

His name was James "Big Man" Maxton, and he showed me his master mosaic, "Angel Alley," designed by Lily Yeh. In a wide alleyway between two of the closed-off streets stood a wall of 15-foot-high angels confronting that whole bleak area with colorful African splendor. It was this work which had transformed him from a drug dealer to an incomparable artisan.

When Big Man's mother died, he was so shocked that he cleared himself of heroin and took many of the things she had loved—old dishes and glasses, photos and frames—and broke them into pieces. Then he cemented them onto a pylon as a monument in her honor and offered his services to his transformational mentor Lily Yeh.

Who was Lily Yeh, this human guardian angel, the founder, the extraordinary spirit behind this transformation of urban blight? She was and still is a quiet and beautiful woman, filled with an intensity of light that easily flows from her to everyone around her. Daughter of a Chinese general under Chiang Kai Chek, she was born in China, brought up in Taiwan, and has lived in the United States for more than 30 years. As an artist, she has earned many awards and scholarships.

How did she start in this place of seeming hopelessness? She said, "I was so scared, I wanted to

Restoration is a way for people to develop a relation with the land.

CHRISTINE SCHNIDER,
URBAN ECOLOGIST

Lily Yeh in front of a mosaic flowering tree in the Village of Arts & Humanities.

leave. But then I thought: *If I don't do this, some light in me dies.* I stayed."

And so, with a $2,000 grant from the Pennsylvania Council of the Arts, Lily started her work in an area recommended by a dancer friend. She began by picking up trash in an empty lot. The first local man to ask what she was up to was Joseph Williams, or Jojo. "Making a place of beauty," she answered. Jojo was silent for a while. Then he said, "I'll go get the children." So he rounded them up and, out of the rubble, they created the first courtyard and, as joyful sentinels, made concrete trees covered with mosaics of broken glass and dishes. Then, pathways were constructed and the first flowers planted.

There is no spot of ground, however arid, bare or ugly, that cannot be tamed into such a state as may give an impression of beauty and delight.

GERTRUDE JEKYLL

Her work crew was from age three-and-a-half to 13 years old. Some of the kids dubbed her, "that crazy Chinese lady." That was in 1988-1989.

During my visit, I asked her why she had envisioned that oasis in that particular place. She replied, "I am a Chinese landscape painter. Do you know that quality of Chinese landscapes that is more than a landscape?" I asked, "Do you mean that atmosphere of light, of spirit, or Zen?" She nodded, "Yes, that ineffable quality. Chinese landscape paintings depict a place known as the 'dustless realm,' a place of pristine beauty and tranquility beyond passions and desires. I tried to find that quality in this country, but I could not. So I tried to help make such a place of beauty—here, in fact. My goal is to establish this 'dustless' place in the community art that we create."

In planning the village's central Meditation Park, she said:

We would like to create a place with a gentle atmosphere, where neighborhood residents can relax and quietly enjoy the company of their friends. It will be a place of reflection, recollection, and spiritual replenishment. At the Village of Arts and Humanities, my work aims to reconnect people, to comfort and to heal.

In order that the park can shelter and, to some extent, seclude the people inside it from street activities outside, we will build a masonry wall that is high enough to create a private world for the people within the park. The wall will have a slightly undulating top so as to create a soft and welcoming feeling. In order to relate the meditation park to our African park, we will cover the wall with plaster and mosaic decorations.

Inside the park, we will create patterns by paving the ground with pebbles, cobblestones, bricks. Open trellis pavilions will be erected to create semi-private spaces in the park. Benches, tables, and lamp-posts will be installed, and trees, bushes and flowers will be planted. We want the atmosphere of the park to be soothing and spacious. Colors and patterns will be chosen carefully to bring liveliness to the place without disturbing its feeling of peace and tranquility.

Transformation of the Village was the work of many hands. Left: Lily Yeh and "Big Man" lay a pathway. Below: Big Man's 15-foot-high master mosaic, "Angel Alley," designed by Lily Yeh, transformed a wide alleyway. Chapter Eight photos courtesy of Lily Yeh.

Artistic creations at the Village of Arts & Humanities

Lily Yeh had left a successful art career as a painter to work on the village. Observers recall that virtually all her work since then, beginning with the clearing and transformation of that first dump lot, has been collaborative, involving local residents. Also involved were invited artists, playwright H. German Wilson, choreographer Lone Nash and many others.

Since then, awards and plaudits have flowed in from all over the world. In common, they celebrate the work of a woman whose background was hardly suggestive of someone who might make a difference in a miserable inner-city neighborhood. She was not a social worker, urban planner, wealthy philanthropist, or business tycoon. She was an artist who came to the U.S. to attend the University of Pennsylvania's School of Fine Arts. Friends and associates have pointed out that the rough and tumble streets of Philadelphia's ghetto must have felt as unfamiliar to her as the landscape of Mars.

As the village grew, other initiatives, such as writing, art, and dance classes, took on lives of their own. Along with small parks and gardens, Lily worked to create a youth theater, where students learned about African folk tales. Although students told of the drugs invading their community and other problems, she helped many local people, nonetheless, find beauty in themselves.

In 2004, Lily left the village to work in many other countries, including China. Anxious to stay involved in leading-edge problems, she also worked in Rwanda, where a massacre had created a mass grave site. Determined that the bereft citizens would never forget what happened there, she got help and, with many community members, dug up the bone chambers and then properly buried the dead found in these chambers. Years later, as a tribute to the Chinese teachers called the Barefoot Artists she created the Barefoot Artists Foundation. With this organization, she encouraged the teaching of migrant workers' children who would otherwise have no schooling.

Her inspired programs have become legendary, and in America, a national model of urban renewal. This is because Lily recognizes the innate artistry, the potential for idealism and caring in neighborhood people all over the world. She gives them love, the tools and knowledge by which they can begin to fulfill themselves, and ignites the spirit of wonder at their accomplishments. This generates

When we find beauty within ourselves, we can become a self-sustaining community. Then we will be able to garden and live from our own vegetable gardens.
LILY YEH

Lily working with Big Man to finish a mosaic mural.

hope and a "We did it" response.

As Lily once said,

We can be inspired to put in a new lamp-post, make an old people's park, clean out another "Love Canal," help those at-risk children. We have the power to elicit and direct change that benefits us. The more our children can participate in this total process of making ourselves responsible, as well as demanding that our elected officers be responsible too, the better preparation these children will have for their future.

Lily Yeh in Rwanda with children and workers who are helping her paint a mural.

The natural world is the larger sacred community to which we belong. To be alienated from this community is to become destitute in all that makes us human. To damage this community is to diminish our own existence.

THOMAS BERRY

Healing of the Whole Earth

CHAPTER NINE

Awakening the Visionary in All of Us

Opening the eyes we see there is no path
But only ways where tendrils
Metamorph in the most delicate prayer
Not yet known to us.

- Excerpted from a poem by John Waddell, 1992

In most of us there is the capacity for powerful intuition, an artistry and a depth of feeling that needs to be awakened and nurtured, to feel the light, the radiance of an idea, pouring through. Shamans, artists, poets, musicians, painters and all people touched by grace, hold the wisdom of the past and the future in their visions. Encourage them to project their knowledge to quicken the spirit and vision in all of us.

And there lies the key: Memories of fragrances, music and touch, in the hands of the artist, the musician and the writer serve to awaken us all—to reach into our souls and whisper or shout in paint or

The man who is tenacious of purpose in a rightful cause is not shaken from his firm resolve by the frenzy of his fellow citizens clamoring for what is wrong or by the tyrant's threatening countenance.

HORACE: 65-8

clay, trumpet or gesture—that this is our world. Therefore, there is an absolute necessity to bear witness to wanton destruction around the globe and to end it.

Television, to be sure, can be a tool for this awakening. Various nature programs, sponsored by the National Geographic Society, the Smithsonian Institute, the Cousteau Society and many environmental groups, have served as forerunners to bring us both the wonders of, and devastations to, the natural world. We see whales, not only as beleaguered and slaughtered victims, but also as playful and sensitive companions, willing to be patted on the head from a boat. We hear the profoundly moving whale songs, and the ultrasound frequencies bring us the calls of dolphins and seals. Through modern technology we

Forty-foot-long humpback whale breaching off the southwest coast of Maui in Hawaii.

have learned to distinguish between mating and danger calls, as well as companion or play voices.

Television makes real for us the fabulous varieties of bird, insect and plant life in the jungles of Brazil or Borneo. We see the protective devices nature has innovated, such as the Viceroy butterfly impersonating the famous Monarch. The Viceroy provides delicious dining for birds, but his involuntary protector, the Monarch, is apparently inedible. Many species of birds, animals and plants have chameleon-like behavior; we know, of course, that in northern climes weasels become white in winter as do some foxes, hares and birds such as ptarmigans.

Television can also show us the physical joy of a raven cavorting in the air or a dolphin leaping in water and the actual smile on an animal's face when it is courting or showing gratitude. Then there is the grief of a baby animal separated from its mother that has been shot, as well as the agony of an animal being used for experiments. Consider, for instance, television shows featuring the robber-baron Japanese, Russian or more recent Norwegian whale-hunters flouting the international whale moratorium and killing "scientific specimens." And celebrate the intrepid heroes in a Greenpeace longboat lying down in the path of the whaler or warning off the whales, or taking other evasive or aggressive action. And celebrate also all the exciting ramifications of the chase, darting in and out of icebergs, or hiding in fiords.

More TV programming could highlight such things as the fascinating drama of the woman who cared passionately about the Brazilian rainforests and made a deal with the U.S. government to reduce Brazil's huge debt to the U.S. in return for stopping some of the cutting of rainforests. It could also pose to viewers: Why can't all the comparatively rich nations help to ransom the rainforests by assuming such debts?

And there's the tale of Sir Edmund Hillary, who built a hospital in Nepal in gratitude to its citizens for their help during his conquest of Mt. Everest, and the subsequent cutting down of the trees for buildings to house the enormous influx of visitors. Then, as the trees were cut, the mountainsides eroded, and the Nepalese lifestyle was threatened. Next, the long road back: Hillary and his guide and

companion, Tenseng, showed the schoolchildren how to plant little trees up and down the mountains.

Moreover, the television programs could offer more dramas or detective stories about the destruction and potential redemption of natural life—situations that have happened. There are, for example, the extraordinary statements of human courage and ingenuity, such as the life story of Dian Fossey, the renowned heroine in *Gorillas in the Mist,* who was murdered for her attempt to protect the gorillas.

Another enormously effective, dramatic plea for world attention—particularly of American concern—is the 2006 movie and book, *An Inconvenient Truth,* by former Vice President Al Gore. The facts about global warming have become more and more evident. The photographs of its devastation—the melting snows on famed glaciers and mountaintops such as Kilimanjaro, Fuji, and the Matterhorn; the melting and splitting of entire major ice shelves in the Antarctic; the drowning of polar bears that can no longer find ice floes to climb onto for safety; the drying up of lakes and rivers worldwide—all indicate the results of our callously ignoring man's impact on nature!

Beyond debate, the world needs to curb the source of carbon dioxide in the atmosphere and the burning of fossil fuels—car exhaust fumes, high smoke emissions from factories and usurping our deep water aquifers for endless development—all of which contribute to the greenhouse atmosphere. The world's people must stop cutting down the forests of the Earth. This causes the drying out of whole continents. We need to *SAVE* our most precious resource of all—*WATER*—the "blue gold" of the world's lifeline.

Most of all, our country needs more leaders, like Al Gore, with the courage and knowledge to galvanize us into an effective force, as well as a critical mass of people willing to change our habits in order for us to survive. To survive we all need to confront these truths.

Once, I saw the paintings by a 14-year-old child that showed creatures perishing in the burning rainforests. Those portraits of a toucan, a jaguar and a jungle butterfly were so immediate, so intense, that they leapt into my heart and consciousness. I thought: How can we bear to let this beauty be destroyed forever? One child's brush had brought the soul of these particular creatures into my awareness, as no statistics—however horrifying—ever could!

What if television and documentaries could share this natural garden of the world as seen through the artistry of a child's eyes? Each whale or seal, lion, lizard, toucan or butterfly could become an individual through a child's paintbrush, action or song. What an education for both child and adult: the child learning first-hand the creatures' names, their habitats, their customs and ways of moving and eating; the adult being reawakened through the child's perception. Both would gain greater understanding of how animals depend on plants, plants depend on soil, water and sun, and soil depends on the waste products of the animal—one of endlessly related cycles of life.

In the contemporary world, the video camera has become a ubiquitous means of communication. It can serve as the unseen watcher, the eavesdropper to capture and hear the direct expression of love a child exclaims when enchanted by an individual, a beauty, a sound, a vision. It can share its record with us in the adult world and we, too, can learn how essential and exciting is this child's sense of the world. Adults would also be reawakened.

Speaking of children's eyes, I watched a group of about 18 children who had come for a weekend of environmental teaching at a camp in an Arizona ponderosa pine forest. Their instructor, Jim Huber, a scientist, has an understanding of ecology and all its intricate ramifications, combined with a love for the outdoors and a gentle sense of humor. He had given them a specific question: How does the animal food-chain work? A general discussion emerged, that focused on what animals eat:

The state of mind that enables a man to do work of this kind is akin to that of the religious worshipper or the lover; the daily effort comes from no deliberate intention or program, but straight from the heart.

ALBERT EINSTEIN
(SAID OF MAX PLANCK)

Some are vegetarian and eat only plants. In this field, what is the most abundant plant?

Grass.

What feeds on grass?

Well, cows?

Yes, but what other kinds of creatures? What could they see feeding on grass, then whirring up into the air?

Why, yes, grasshoppers.

Yes. And what feeds on grasshoppers?

Well, mice?

Yes.

Foxes? Snakes?

Yes, all of them do. Does anyone know what a shrew is? A funny little animal that loves to eat grasshoppers. And what feeds on shrews and mice and snakes?

Owls? Wolves? Hawks?

Yes!

So let's divide up and be some of the creatures. Does it take a few grasshoppers or lots of grasshoppers to eat all that grass?

Lots.

OK, we need ten grasshoppers—who will be grasshoppers? And what do they do? (Show me.)

(Much jumping and chomping.)

Now, do we need as many shrews? No, because, otherwise, there'd be no more grasshoppers. So we need six shrews – hands? And what do the shrews do? Show me.

(Much creeping and crunching of grasshoppers.)

OK, who eats the shrews?

Yes. The hawks!

(Turning to the last children) You two be the hawks.

Now I'll give you ten minutes. The grasshoppers can hop anywhere; the shrews have to try to catch them; and the hawks have to try to catch the shrews. After ten minutes we all stop and see who has caught whom.

For ten minutes happy bedlam reigned. Seven grasshoppers were caught by shrews while four shrews, in turn, were caught by triumphant hawks—and, most importantly, some grasshoppers and shrews were left for future hunts. Not one of the 18 children will ever forget what a food-chain is all about.

I imagine teachers working with young people to care for the Earth in all its wondrous dimensions: to see it, photograph or draw its live creatures; to smell its fragrance under leaves, in marshes and by the sea or after rain; to touch it, dig and plant in it; to hear its bird songs, its spring peepers, its locusts, its winds and waves; to feel it as the dance of living energy in all one's being.

My musician friend, Ani Williams, is a player of many instruments obtained from far countries, including harps, flutes, ocarinas, drums, rattles and didgeridoos. When she goes to a school classroom, she lets the children hear and play each instrument and discover what plant or animal it is made from and what sounds it makes.

In the jungles of Peru, flute players imitate bird calls, animal roars or whines; in Australia, an aborigine's didgeridoo calls for miles across the wild desert land; in Africa, tribes talk to each other on drums. The ram's horn becomes a way of reaching across mountains; the bamboo reed fills the heart with birdsong and the whirring of insects. Music becomes a means of enchantment by which the habits and properties of particular animals and plants are learned. Song is the *lingua franca,* the language of communication between humans and the natural world.

Ani describes one of her adventures in the classroom:

We are nature— long have we been absent, and now we return.
WALT WHITMAN

With drum began the heartbeat, walking through class, making contact with each child; I was hunched over, bent with pain and heaviness as the heart of Mother Earth. I told them I needed their help—I felt something was very wrong, and I needed them to help me know what it was.

Spontaneously, they called out the things they felt were keeping me bent over in pain: pollution, fighting in the families, lack of love, cutting the trees, garbage, were some.

I began to feel better knowing what was wrong; my back straightened up more, all the while, beating the heartbeat on the drum, walking back and forth through the classroom. Then I called for solutions. What can solve some of these problems on the Earth? One young boy called out, "Laws to limit the cutting of trees. Limit the cutting of trees to three a year." Another called, "More music in our homes," (referring to live participatory music played by the family, since we had just finished with 30 minutes of playing various instruments). Another said, "More love in our families," and yet another called for recycling.

So we created a chant to the Earth Mother, including the problems and solutions, all of which came from these children who were about seven years of age.

Ani Williams

Can artists save the planet? A lot of them are trying—at least trying to make it more livable. As adults they are managing to keep alive their sense of wonder. Indeed, some awakened artists are devising new ways of dealing with environmental problems. They work with their communities and they advise, revise and create solutions. Following is a quote from the summer 1989 issue of *Art News* in an article titled, "The Greening of the Art World, the Ecological Revolution."

These days, even a casual chat with many artists can become quickly intimidating. They describe imperiled ecosystems and what's happening with the ozone layer. They list endangered species of birds and butterflies. They can tell you what's poisoning our water and how many redwoods were chopped down last year. They know what's in our garbage, where it goes, and how long it takes to disintegrate. The more they know, the more worried they get. "I feel we have a very short time to save the planet," says New York artist Mierle Ukeles. "The more scientists I talk to, the more I'm convinced of this."

Ukeles works with New York's Department of Sanitation on garbage and recycling programs. One of her goals has been to help the sanitation workers have pride in their work, rather than feeling diminished by the judgment of others.

For his part, Minnesota artist Viet Ngo formed his own corporation to create innovative wastewater treatment systems that are not only effective but handsome. Designed in geometric or curving shapes, his lagoons look beautiful from the air, with cleansing agents of algae and duckweed spread in green patterns. Other artists are designing parks with lakes and walkways where formerly stood a swamp or brook clogged with debris. Still others use recycled materials in the development of huge reforested parks, golf courses over strip-mines and furniture. Recently, Susan Geer convinced 100 people to join her in cleaning up the Los Angeles River, and Dominique Mazaud has led a monthly ceremony to rid the Rio Grande of some of its pollution.

This save-the-planet sensibility is spreading internationally. Artists are gathering garbage from Japan's seashore, planting trees in Germany and creating wildlife habitats in England. In Brazil, the National Movement of Artists for Nature protests the killing of whales and the destruction of indigenous savannas—with their slogan, "Art before it's too late."

To me, another artist's work represents a symbol of our microcosm. Betsy Damon constructed an environment in an exhibition room: a huge canyon of rocks, each of which she and her children had picked out, hauled in and placed in the semblance of a watercourse from the top of one wall all the way across the floor of the room.

The only thing missing was the life force: water.

We, as people, as artists, are also watercourses. What forces of compassion run through us!

We need artists to help us come together and share our voices and build community around powerful issues concerning our roles in the world and our planet's survival. Compassion must be translated into action.

NATASHA MAYERS

Here are two stories of other transformative artists that also support planetary awareness: one, the saga of Vijali Hamilton; the other, the tale of the late Michael Kahn and Lida Levant, a husband-wife team of painter-sculptor-weavers. All of these unique individuals have sown extraordinary beauty in their personal gardens to share with all.

One day, a friend in Santa Fe asked me to meet a dear friend of hers, and that's how I met Vijali Hamilton, a petite, vibrant woman with a mass of red-gold hair and a lovely countenance. She had been part of a Vedanta community of nuns and was a sculptor with gallery contacts. However, a tradition of serving evoked in her a desire to break away from the commercial world and to help communities. She worked for six years in the mountains of California with an indigenous tribe, carving into and painting a rocky cliffside as an interpretation of the beliefs of the people.

Then, Vijali decided to expand her world of monumental sculptures and reach out to more people. So she chose an arbitrary longitudinal line around the globe and visited twelve countries along this line: Italy, Greece, Israel, India, Tibet, and Japan, to name a few, calling her mission, "The World Wheel."

Previously, I had seen some slides of contemporary transformative art. One in particular remained in my mind: a bare mountaintop with an enormous oval ring of blue stones surrounding a ring of white, then gray—the background for a reddish-purple stone cross. It was so vast, so simple. Years later I learned that this was Vijali's conception.

In each country she heard, by word of mouth, where to go next and what community to serve. She listened, then asked these three questions:

- Where do you come from? (Meaning, what are your own and your culture's central beliefs?)
- What is your major "dis-ease" of today?
- How would you best heal this 'dis-ease' if you could?

The answer each community gave became the basis for her healing sculpture and also for a dedication ceremony that is a ritual drama. Both were an exorcism of the "dis-ease," leading to healing.

Vijali Hamilton's artwork inside Tibetan cave

It may take a few months, or even years, to complete each transformation, but in each country something amazing transpired, except in Egypt, where she was personally attacked, but then found refuge in a nearby Coptic monastery. In China, Vijali was warned that she would never be allowed to work, but she so charmed the high officials that they gave her permission to work in any of their national parks. In Tibet, at an altitude of 10,000 feet, Vijali worked with a group of nuns in a mountain cave. Each day became an active prayer, for both physical and spiritual survival. In response to the sisters' silent evocations, she sculpted a seated shadow figure.

She is now embarking on a second "world wheel" in the Southern Hemisphere, having created a base camp meeting place and retreat for her friends around the world in Moab, Utah—a garden oasis for the spirit.

This last story moves to the Arizona high desert. It is the tale of two transplanted Provincetown, Massachusetts, artists, Michael Kahn and Lida Livant, who, originally from New York City, packed their canvasses and belongings into an old truck and came west to Sedona. There they found work as caretakers on a 140-acre property. Out of the white limestone rocks, the blue river shale, lava and yellow sandstone, from the bent mesquite trunks and river driftwood, they created a poignant and strange womb-chapel. They fashioned iridescent rose windows from broken slivers of colored glass, which were glued to under-plates of glass held amongst the patterns of twisting branches and tree trunks.

Michael and Leda Kahn

Today Michael's work casts rainbows across the mosaic stone floors, and a wall of interwoven wood and fragmented twigs hides a doorway into a storage area holding Michael's life work of paintings. His way of creating remained integral to his lifestyle: the weaving together of a vast mosaic of influences, colors, sounds, fragrances, gardens and celebrations. Through his work, his whole life can be seen as a continuum.

An old piano which was built into the wall of the womb-chapel, and a series of unstrung and broken instruments,

The soul should always stand ajar, ready to welcome the ecstatic experience.
EMILY DICKINSON

waited for visitors to play their inner music. Sometimes the cacophony was horrendous but, at other times, everyone felt freed by the radiant harmony of this place. And the sounds became music.

This three-dimensional dream of these two painters represents a unique and ephemeral work of art. Wind and spring floods, as well as sun and time, have transformed the creations and the people who have lived with Michael and Lida, as well as the artists who see their work. One monument of huge driftwood debris from a the river that evolved, flourished and collapsed, has now been replaced by an underground gallery, called Pipe Dreams. Gophers wreak havoc in the vegetable gardens, and weeds sometimes bury the stones. The two artists don't live there anymore,[1] but the spirit of what they have made, given and shared reflects the essence of what human beings can be and how they can transform everything around them into a rhapsody of what is possible.

---

[1] Michael died in 2007; his wife, Lida, moved to Santa Fe in 2009 with their paintings. Eliphante is now protected by caretakers and a gifted friend who hopes it can be maintained as a teaching center.

ELIPHANTE

Can we not see the universe
in all its intricacy of multitudinous invention
Here
in this microcosm of being?
These stained-glass prisms
                of disseminated love
reach into all of our vulnerabilities –
scar
with their proximity
                of luminous stars
a million light years, God to now.
This instant, in this immediate planet's sun,
we live again
                reshaped in time.
The colors wash our tears
into an ocean of primordial radiance.
Is each cathedral of man's aspirations
transient?
And if so, can he form again
this substance of transcendent power
out of his bones?
You have, humble creators, sculpted time
into this Chapel of the Womb
and we are reborn rainbows
                entering light.

The womb-chapel, Eliphante

115

Making Change Happen

How do we personally make changes and evoke the capacity for visions in each of us?

Personally, I pray for the grace of a living prayer to allow me to move with spirit and to create. A living prayer is recognition of beauty, a sense of absolute wonder. Suddenly one is moved, touched, shocked and transformed by something unexpectedly beautiful: a field of wildflowers, waves laughing at a cliff, the sheen of a peony petal, a human face or voice or hands, a body in movement! One becomes a particular passage in music, lives in the cadence of words, leaps or dives or sings into the beauty of a new perception; divinity is touched in a beloved one's physical embrace.

An example of this is a memory from many years ago, the startling vision of Dame Edith Stilwell mounting the stage of New York City's YWCA. She glided forward, clad in a black gown with a train trailing behind, her hands outstretched, each finger encircled in a gigantic ring. Her very high forehead was like an Elizabethan dome, surmounted by the most enormous black hat with the widest brim I had ever seen. Everyone in the room sat up. Her presence was electrifying. There was not a sound in the room. And then, when she spoke, each syllable was so clearly pronounced that one never strained to hear her words; therefore, her poetry could flow into one unimpeded. One became that poetry for an enchanted period out of time.

For each person, perhaps, psychic change is analogous to "Small is Beautiful." People are combining resources to undertake any project where there is love and will: barn-raising a house; building a skating rink, a theatre, a day care center, nursery school or playground; planting and maintaining a garden. Small groups are forming teams to teach, to fund raise, cook, plant seeds, make a video or mural, form a union or a business. As long as people take the initiative themselves to dream, plan and execute their projects, they are self-reliant; they do not need governments or corporations to direct or impose restrictions on small actions. If self-imposed limitations are reasonable and people work to fulfill their dream, they can undertake and complete any self-help project, thereby affirming a sense of dignity, self-worth and accomplishment.

It is not enough to just love nature or want to be in relation to Gaia. Our relation takes place in a place. And it must be grounded in experience and information.
GARY SNYDER

WOODLAND IN AUTUMN

By evoking their nurturing qualities, people can promote new projects by talking to neighbors, town councilors, lawyers, conservation societies, politicians and bankers and by taking time and giving volunteer energy to smooth the way for such undertakings. In fact, they often do that already. Garden club members share their knowledge, expertise, materials and funding, where necessary, with their neighbors. Beyond that, people can oversee the working conditions of migrant laborers who come to harvest crops; this may involve a process of persuading officials and owners to provide safe, attractive and bearable living quarters for these workers and their families.

However, it often takes a catalyst to convey the intense necessity to act and together to reach a solution. Such a catalyst can be a naturalist or scientist, an artist, an engineer, a teacher, anyone dedicated to finding a solution.

As an example, the extraordinary woman, Jane Goodall, succeeded in changing many misconceptions about chimpanzees and animals in general, such as, animals cannot use tools; they do not suffer (in cages, in laboratories enduring countless tortures); and humans cannot learn much from them. For many years she lived with chimpanzees in the wild, watching them use plant stems as tools to prod termite heaps and draw out the succulent termites onto the stems. She learned that each chimpanzee has a distinct personality and can show great love and caring for its young and for members of its traveling group. She also discovered that each one can, on occasion, become enraged and commit murder and atrocious acts on other apes.

By visiting zoos and labs all over the world, she learned that animals are often driven to despair or horror, apathy or dread by mankind's actions, like shooting mother chimpanzees to kidnap babies for sale to experimental laboratories. There, they are often incarcerated and imprisoned for years.

Goodall created a foundation in her name to provide funds to keep existing bands alive, prevent poaching and help preserve and expand habitats. Her understanding of the suffering of so many natural species has led to numerous lectures and meetings to help change attitudes and to establish educational groups, such as, "Roots and Shoots," to nurture and inculcate young children with love of nature and all its beings. She believes that, since our young are our invested hope for the future, there is the need to encourage each individual so that all people learn that they have the means to feel the needs of all living creatures and to protect them.

It was Rachel Carson who wrote about the consequences of certain pesticides that affected all forms of life along the food chain, from microorganisms in the sea and land to fish, plant life, animals and birds—and eventually to us. Few people believed her until they saw whole flocks of robins keel over because of lethal accumulations of DDT in the earthworms they were eating, or riversides strewn with dead fish, also victims of toxic doses of pesticides in their diets. She became a maligned Cassandra at hands of the chemical companies, but eventually public opinion and the courts forced DDT out of the domestic marketplace.

The late Jacques Cousteau was another catalyst. He took action on behalf of diminished marine wildlife, threatened by oil spills and ubiquitous drift nets throughout the oceans. John Muir and Eliot Porter preserved our heritage of wilderness, by action and artistry, echoing other voices. By building seed banks to guard plant species, by reforesting devastated areas and cleaning the seas, rivers and

Once burgeoning life along coral reef

Every moment nature starts on the longest journey, and every moment she reaches her goal.

GOETHE

skies, ways exist to change our attitudes and actions. If we infuse the souls of the natural world into our minds, our lives and our hearts, then we can feel that these are the living fellow creatures whose world we share.

Beyond that, we need to feel in our bones the rising anguish of the bones of the Earth. We need to see and feel our own blood poured out and wasted like the water from deep aquifers. The pollutants we take into our veins are the drugs that mask our own capacities to feel and act. We need to weep again, be

Child creating chalk painting on sidewalk

cleansed and to have our selves filled with glowing dreams. We need to heed *Silent Spring* through the static. We need to know how whales are faring. Today is the genocide of the Leviathan.

The question is, where do such catalysts come from—nature, teachers, life itself? For example, children fortunate enough to have inspired art teachers can find the inherent glory of color. Perhaps they can discover a kind of salvation in art.

Children who begin their earth studies or life studies do not experience any numinous *aspect of these subjects. The excitement of existence is diminished. If this fascination, this entrancement, with life is not evoked, the children will not have the psychic energies needed to sustain the sorrows inherent in the human condition. They might never discover their true place in the vast world of time and space. Teaching children about the natural world should be treated as one of the most important events in their lives. Children need a story that will bring personal meaning of the universe.*

- Thomas Berry, *The Dream of the Earth*,
University of California Press, Sierra Club Books, 1988

They are our children, in America, a microcosm of the world. Wherever they might be—in Europe, Asia, the Middle East, Russia or Africa—are they finding their inner gardens?

120

TO SERVE

Sing to us in prisms of Your incandescent light
    and call our name
      in madrigals of opal, emerald, jade!
For we are the diverse-toned tesserae
    Of mosaicked choice
    with which to form
          new tapestries of mind
    across cathedral naves…
we, and all equal quality of beings,
    which You shall garner
        to serve.
You can recognize us in dust:
we are particles of bent sun
    suspended in both memory and heart.
We are the transformed future
    culled from the leavings, discards

      of all random acts
to be designed by diamond drills
    into the jeweled tiaras of Your vision.
These beacons, towers
    gleaned from all broken promises and hopes
      are Yours to fashion
    leaning into light of distant years.
Carry us as fractals of Your love
      in quiet reunion:
blood on bone and tissue of each star-lit soul
    in magnified dimension…
      each pattern unique.
We are the rainbowed remnants of the universe
    gathered
    to be recreated
      and to serve.

CHAPTER TEN

Protecting the Garden of Earth

The root of our most modern sin—we do not love the earth enough.

- Erik Reece (Kentucky Teacher)

A garden may become an image of self-healing and a means of drawing together small communities of people. As a metaphor, the garden can be extended to the healing of the whole Earth. Indeed, firing up our hearts to accomplish the redeeming of the Earth will require enlightened imagination and action by the visionary in all of us.

Facing these challenges will require more people with clear missions to produce cleaner waters, pure air, closed holes in the ozone layer, restored forests and grasslands, as well as marshes and farmlands free of pesticides. Together, they must confront these challenges and change their attitudes so that they may find alternative, Earth-harmonious ways to produce food, energy and building materials—and stop wasting and destroying natural resources and start protecting more species of living creatures. To do this, we need overall global planning and training at all levels: international, governmental, community and individual.

In her enthralling book, *Bring Me the Ocean*, Roberta Reynolds Cooper describes her way of bringing entire environments of plants into a hospital complex. She and her helpers lugged stones,

What is the vitality and necessity of clean water? Ask the man who is ill, who is lifting his lips to the cup. Ask the forest.

MARY OLIVER

sand or earth, mosses, ferns, small trees, marsh cattails—whatever was appropriate for a particular site to create a living setting. A small barrier enclosed these environments, which were mounted on a plastic sheet; the children could see the objects and also touch, smell and hold them. Roberta engaged them in discussion: animals, birds, insects that lived in this particular environment; what they ate; how they felt if something destroyed their home; and what they could do, such as painting or writing about them. The hospital patients often identified with different aspects: sometimes a fragrance or touch would open up a flood of memories and accelerate healing.

Beyond that, on a global scale we face equally enormous and dramatic challenges to rebuild and heal our planet. The increase of greenhouse gases and air pollution worldwide poses just one of these

many challenges. For example, it is only too obvious when flying from one continent to another, that the mass of air pollution is a solid band encircling the world.

How could the Impressionists or Van Gogh have painted their immortal sun-drenched worlds under today's polluted gray skies? The trouble is, when people live with thickening skies and oily waters day by day, they feel powerless in the face of polluters. These are people who have never caught a fish or enjoyed a bird's song. They have not learned that wild animals have feelings just as they do.

Recently, some citizens of Mexico City visited Santa Fe to attend a conference. After dinner at a private home one evening, the guests disappeared outdoors. Their hostess was understandably perplexed and worried that her dinner had been a failure. But when they came back, they were all smiling and excited. "Oh," they cried, "we have been looking at the stars! We haven't seen them for years!"

Without doubt, the possibilities of the Earth's rehabilitation are abundant, but it will take persistence and courage in the face of insult and danger from those with vested interests who are fighting change. It will also take courage to track down the poachers who attack and mutilate the rhinoceroses, elephants and walruses for bone and ivory, to find those who capture gorillas and chimpanzees for zoos and to expose companies that dump toxic wastes into our backyards, rivers and oceans. It will take further courage to stop the legal double-talk that the strip-mining and anti-environmental forces tack onto referendums and bills, under the guise of protecting property rights!

How strange and wonderful is our home, our earth.
EDWARD ABBEY

To tell the truth, it will take time and enormous energy to rebuild, reforest and rehabilitate the Earth. An important step is to accelerate waste recycling programs. Fresh evidence of recycling appears everywhere in the world as it becomes increasingly clear that we are using up our cheap mineral resources, and landfills are bulging. Recycled paper helps to save the world's forests. Recycled plastics, combined with recycled wood or paper (such as the product made under the trade name Trex®), make decking and floorboards more maintenance-free than wood itself. Bottles, melted down, will again yield pure glass; pure iron can be retrieved from the automobile graveyards; all kinds of metal scraps can be converted to steel—and to art.

Enlightened companies have the opportunity to become industry leaders. For example, not only

ALLOY (to Simon Rodia)

Your blow-torch blast
     can fuse and sear
     scald molten metals
          into one
and write a flaming God-shape clear
     in bronze or iron
          tin aluminum or gold.

The very chaos
     of constructed form
     can catch
          the unused poetry
of a function
can isolate the strength of girders
     spans and aerials   high wire
          and cranes
transform
this malleable potential
          into welded song.

does the Stone Container Company on Arizona's Mogollon Rim recycle paper and cardboard, but also any remaining water from the process is filtered into a newly created pool in the nearby forest, attracting wildlife such as deer, elk and many animal and bird species—some even considered vanished. They have re-created a habitat and performed a useful function—and made it profitable. In that vein, the Ben and Jerry Ice Cream Company found that recycling ice cream containers could save more than one million dollars per year.

A wonderful prototype for recycled art is the Watts Towers in Los Angeles. The sculptor, Simon Rodia, was a poor Italian immigrant and mason. So enamored was he of his foster country that he created a love poem, influenced by findings in the Los Angeles junk yards: broken shards of glass and china, discarded steel chassis of old automobiles, plus sticks and stones. From 1921 through 1954, he transformed these materials into strangely poignant cathedral towers. During the 1968 Watts riots, these monuments were among the only buildings left standing. They were protected by citizens of that area. Although damaged during the 1994 Northridge earthquake, the towers have been repaired and stand today in a small

neighborhood park, Rodia's memory still revered.

I also remember the lovely true story written by Elzeard Bouffier. It is a story about Jean Giono who planted acorns in the waterless, barren, denuded hills above a certain deserted town in France to live. Each night, in his small hut, he soaked acorns in water to stimulate their growth; then during the day he would lovingly insert them into the earth across the hills and valley.

The poetry of earth is ceasing never.
JOHN KEATS

Gradually, these grew and became a visible forest where no one expected it. Finally, streams began to flow again; birds and animals found sustenance; and the small town, with running water once again, drew people back. A whole valley became productive and alive.

By now we should have increased our elation and thankfulness for the wonders of nature. Instead, we have lost much of our love and happiness. We must lift ourselves again high above our microscopes, telescopes, books, newspapers, and computers and see again the total beauty of a flower, a brook, of a woman, of a child, of the world, of the stars. Yes, our miraculous planet Earth should irradiate human thankfulness and joy, into every direction of the universe.

- Robert Muller

CHAPTER ELEVEN

Passive and Active Healing

Healing is a matter of time, but it is also a matter of opportunity.

- Hippocrates (450 BC – 377 BC)

When people become overwhelmed by stress or worry, they often end up in a hospital—frequently a noisy, sterile environment humming with mechanistic methods for curing, from radiation and chemotherapy to MRIs and CT scans. Owing to the efforts of citizen groups and artists, however, some hospitals have created gardens, sunrooms and solariums. Once there, patients may allow the beauty and fragrances of plants to envelop them. Just such a transformation may be seen within the Good Samaritan Hospital in Phoenix, Arizona, on what was once an acre of cement.

"Good Sam" patients find themselves in a blossoming paradise, busy with wildflowers, desert bushes and trees in a glorious profusion of colors, shapes and textures. A small waterfall leads into a number of water channels that follow the tiers of cement borders for flower beds, following the curves of the tiers. Each is shaped like a miniature mountain stream, filled with colored borders in a kaleidoscope of desert colors: mauve, orange, sienna, pale grays, whites and yellows. Adjacent to the channels, enclosed by a shallow edging, are wide seats so that patients and visitors can relax, talk, be silent or trail their fingers in the water. Rather than a patient being confronted with blank, dark walls, imagine a festival of mosaic tiles in scarlet, sapphires, emeralds, and gold, leaping around each base with inspirational words intermingled among tiles of varying sizes.

Good Samaritan courtyard garden nearing completion.

The inspired creators of this garden at "Good Sam" include Christy TenEyck, a famed Phoenix landscape architect; Joan Baron, a mosaicist and ceramic artist; Barbara Crisp, the architect; and Joe Taylor, sculptor of the garden's wrought-iron gateway. From design to completion, the garden took six years, a time during which hospital authorities, doctors, nurses, patients and construction workers were consulted and became participants in the design. This transformation reaffirms what healers from every century have known. Gardens are living creations of beauty, bringing fragrances and colors into everyday consciousness, providing quiet, peace and, most of all, joy.

Unfortunately, such opportunities for passive healing are not commonplace. In today's world physicians and their patients, insurance companies, legislative bodies and, in truth, the public at large, have not recognized either the need for or the benefits of passive healing. Nor do they acknowledge the role of gardens, though they do speak of the merits of preventative medicine, which primarily is limited to tests, herbs and vaccinations. Today, most people rely on measurable proof of healing: the killing of a certain number of cancer cells, fevers dropping to normal, or organs and body parts being removed or restored. While often appropriate, the healing capacities of patients—through prayer, contact with living creatures and growing plants—are not widely recognized.

Christy TenEyck

The late George O'Callaghan, a onetime California publisher, suffering from a heart condition, might have had a different moment at the time of death. Peering out from his hospital window, he eyed a rooftop busy with pipes, coolers and huge generators. "It was the last view he ever had," recalls his widow, Madeleine. "What if the rooftop had been busy with flowers, gardens and fountains and a sign reading, WELCOME?"

In the oncology wing of the Sedona, Arizona, Medical Center, Gardens for Humanity followed the example of landscape designer, Topper Delauny. During chemotherapy treatment for a severe bout of cancer, it is rumored that she swore: "If I ever survive from this, I am going to persuade this hospital to give its cancer patients something better to look at than a blank wall! They need something living to help them heal!" She did survive and successfully designed a healing garden filled with plant varieties thought to help cure cancer. These plants include Madagascar Periwinkle, used for treatment of leukemia; May Apple, poisonous when green, not edible when fully ripe, used for treating tumors; the Yew, which produces taxol, for ovarian cancer and some forms of brain cancer. What's more, she created a quiet, contemplative garden where anxious patients could watch plants grow, read how each plant is used for healing and feel some rejuvenating force calm their inner fears.

Imitating Topper Delauny's idea, Gardens for Humanity made a cancer garden in Sedona. To our surprise, we learned that the one thing that distracted our local patients from their misery was seeing a

*Where flowers bloom
so does hope.*
LADY BIRD JOHNSON

roadrunner, an energetic desert bird in action. So bird feeders and flowers were added among the sculpted dwarf fruit trees.

Today, the news is that more hospitals, nursing homes and rehabilitation centers are beginning to turn to gardens for healing. Why not make space for the sun and wind, for flowers, for water, to listen to and touch? Perhaps nature and beauty can actually reach inner places that radium and chemotherapy cannot, thus providing a tactile message of hope.

Indeed, the whole future of healing medicinal gardens could be discussed on a much larger scale, with particular herbs, shrubs and trees planted for treatment of illnesses other than cancer. Echinacea, for example, is a large daisy-like flower, now used to increase immunity to colds and a variety of sicknesses, boils, shingles, fevers. So many other herbs—lobelia, yarrow, hyssop, St. John's Wort—are used in various forms of medical and homeopathic healing.

Echinacea flowers in full bloom

Consider this story. In an urban hospital, a small boy of nine years was fighting leukemia, and his past two years had been a constant hell of hospitalization: tests, treatments and chemotherapy. Although he had been offered distractions, such as books, drawing materials and videos, he wanted none of these. He pleaded, "I want something alive. Everything here is closed around me. Nothing moves! I want to see something grow."

So his mother brought him seeds and earth to put into tiny pots in the hospital. When he was allowed to go home, they transferred the seedlings to bigger pots, then to the garden. Little by little he saw his garden blossom. Soon he was healed.

Hospitals aside, there are other ways in which gardens may be instrumental in creating preventative medicine, or active rather than passive healing. For instance, when an art therapist actively engages in practicing therapy with patients in a garden setting, the beneficial effect over a period of time can be dramatic; not only is the patient surrounded by the fragrances and ambiance of the garden but is painting, writing or dancing out his or her troubles.

One such art therapist is Ellen Speert of Encinitas, California. She brings patients to her garden, providing them with an atmosphere of radiant beauty in which to paint in peace. Gradually, over a period of weeks or months, the patients absorb this green healing. Their pictures change as the patients come ever closer to the causes of their trauma, until there is resolution. One might argue that this process of painting is what truly heals the patient. But Speert feels that the garden itself, by its own living energy, offers the necessary stimulus and helps to speed the healing process.

Among art therapists, there is a growing group of practitioners who are expanding their expertise by community ventures, such as Store-Front Healing Centers. These offer sanctuaries for street people—addicts, homeless and the mentally ill—the tragic denizens of our culture, who have been lost in wastelands.

One of the most enlightened teachers, Janet Timm-Botis, works in her imaginatively renovated workshop in an impoverished area in downtown Albuquerque. She offers her walk-in customers coffee and edibles and presents them with a variety of projects of multi-colored shapes, using paper, fiber, cardboard, wood or metal. From these they can prod, paint, form and manipulate their designs. Some of these handiworks become usable articles: frames, pictures, placemats, sculptured boxes and benches. Just as important are the smiles, the sense of belonging, the pride in making something and the satisfaction of self-empowerment. It is the process of creating—no matter what the product—that heals.

In Wellesley, Massachusetts, another special garden was commissioned by the director of the Institute for Child and Adolescent Development, Sebantiano Santostefano. The goal: to heal deeply disturbed children. Named the Therapeutic Garden for Children, it won, in 1997, the landscape design profession's top honor for its creator, Douglas Reed. Within the lush area of trees, bushes and rolling lawns are quiet, provocative places for children: a stream; a cave; and a bridge of stepping stones across a grassy rill; an island thicket of shrubs; a high mound to help build confidence; and a glade for running and playing.

Delightful and different surprises help each child to fantasize. Some would call the child's behavior active healing, but others still believe the garden itself offers passive healing. Douglas Reed says, "There is increased interest in incorporating gardens and landscape that relieves stress and provides a refuge so that a person can restore one's emotional and physical health."

All over the country, more and more examples of active healing are receiving scientific and legislative scrutiny. Thomas G. Amason, Jr., M.D., a pediatrician who practices in Birmingham, Alabama, is a staunch member of the American Horticultural Therapy Association. He believes that, "Through collective efforts it has now been successfully proven that horticultural therapy is a rewarding therapeutic modality for people with physical impairment, mental retardation, emotional disturbances, behavioral disorders, learning disabilities, and poor social skills or self-esteem."

In the 1970's, Kansas State University created the first degree program in Horticultural Therapy in the United States. Other universities have also started to recognize that a positive relationship between people and plants is therapeutic. And, in 1984, a Developmental Disabilities Act and Education of Handicapped Children Amendments authorized funds to implement actual programs in horticultural therapy.

In addition to this legislation, opportunities exist for pediatricians to encourage home-planting projects to teach a child to nurture plants, produce flowers, fruits and vegetables. The simple sharing of flowers grown from seeds or seedlings, or tomatoes from a single tomato plant, gives a child the feeling of accomplishment and recognition that he/she is capable of producing something of communal value.

Today, there are other government funds available to help at-risk children, those exposed to violence, drugs, negligence and family turmoil. Often their psychological and physical health are in real peril, even their very lives, from suicide or murder. Daily we hear of the threat to students in urban communities, particularly those whose parents work and who have no place to go after school.

However, Boys and Girls Clubs, Scouts and sports clubs offer programs to prevent or at least mitigate the constant threats to students left alone after school; here and there an enlightened teacher will present opportunities for drama or music, painting or dance as a lifeline. But it is rare that political officials or police acknowledge or recognize the therapeutic values of these arts or of gardening. The examples which prove how much help these provide are rarely recorded, because teachers and students are involved in the action of doing, not counting statistics or judging. Even so, schools are beginning to include gardening as an active part of their curricula, relating it to science, art and even economics classes.

Yet another kind of active healing occurs in areas where concerned citizens and federal programs are healing the Earth by extracting toxic wastes from it. One example is "The Revival Field" in Pigs-Eye Landfill in Minnesota, where artist Mel Chin and research agronomist Rufus Claney are practicing green remediation. Plants that can absorb heavy metals, called hyper-accumulators, can tolerate these heavy metals and store them in roots and stems. Examples of these plants include turnips which assimilate lead, potatoes that absorb uranium and saltbush that holds lead.

When fully grown, many different species, such as fescue grasses, corn, romaine, bladder campion and alpine penny grass, were laid out like a target in circles and burned when fully grown. They were planted to cleanse the toxic materials of zinc and cadmium from industrial waste and car batteries. The metals were retrieved from the ashes and sold to defray the costs—an extraordinarily cheap way of dealing with toxic hazards! A complete recycling!

In this kind of healing we can employ the environmental arts. Cleansing pollution from rivers and ponds, rehabilitating whole areas devastated by strip-mining, and reforesting logged areas are vital for the restoration of ecological balance.

The question is: Is America up to it?

Everybody needs beauty as well as bread, places to play in and pray in, where nature may heal and give strength to body and soul alike.

JOHN MUIR

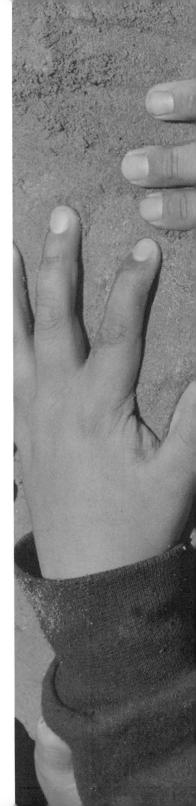

CHAPTER TWELVE

Gardens for Humanity

The world today is sick to its thin blood for lack of elemental things,
for fire before the hands, for water welling from the earth,
for air, for the dear earth itself underfoot.

- Henry Beston from the Outermost House (1928)

n 1995, a group of artists, educators and volunteers—all passionate gardeners—banded together to form a group called Gardens for Humanity (GfH). Their mission was to create gardens of healing with appropriate art. They visualized building and teaching in versions of vest-pocket parks on empty city dump lots, in schools, hospitals, jails and on tribal reservations. Everywhere, the silent radiance and fragrance of the flowers would offer subtle and transforming magic.

However, while the theories sounded fine on paper and in discussion, they did not have a track record or public exposure. Fortunately, an opportunity arose when GfH was given a gifted and guiding hand by the principal of the Lowell Elementary School in Phoenix, Arizona, (with a 75 percent Hispanic population). This principal, Alice Trujillo, was initiating a curriculum with ecology and gardens at its center. She welcomed GfH's help in transforming an acre of cement into wildflower gardens with desert

Planting an apple tree in Karmapa's Peace Garden in Sedona.

trees and shrubs, a fish pond and a ramada with columns, onto which we helped the students design mosaic patterns. It took six years and the devoted hands of many other groups to retrain her teachers and stimulate and inspire the students and parents alike. Also, she had to convince city authorities that her efforts were not only effective but praiseworthy. For this project she won the first citywide award for environmental excellence from Arizona Valley Forward Association.

Also, GfH built a demonstration healing garden in cooperation with Phoenix's Maricopa County Cooperative Extension Service. Its designer, Aimee Beth Ward,[1] oversaw the formidable task of laying water pipes and electric lines, preparing soil for planting healing plants such as aloe vera, mullein, echinacea, mint, valerian, calendula, borage, desert poppies and mesquite trees. She persuaded local volunteers, as well as nearby companies and universities, to provide services. Ward taught visiting school students how to build earth adobe walls using mud and hay bales and decorating them with murals and found objects. Finishing this project took two years and has become a teaching garden for Master Gardeners of the Extension Service.

Other opportunities for school gardens have opened up over those 14 years— in Flagstaff, Verde Valley and Sedona, Arizona; also in Massachusetts, Maine, South Dakota and Washington State. Altogether GfH created or founded gardens in numerous schools, urban housing projects and sanctuaries, on the Navajo and Lakota reservations and in several healthcare facilities. Furthermore, GfH worked with City of Sedona authorities and other institutions on two occasions: one, to make a contemplative corner within a small botanical park and, secondly, to create

---

[1] See Appendix, p. 188.

a memorial garden named for Sedona Schnebly, an early pioneer.

Perhaps the most successful joint venture was with the founder of the Sedona Creative Life Center, Shirley Caris, to create a garden at the Center to honor the 17th Karmapa of Tibet, His Holiness Gwalwa Karmapa Ogyen Trinley Dorje (see page 145). From across the world, we heard that he wanted us to create a "natural garden with an apple tree."

Then, in Sedona, GfH worked in three public schools both in a Head Start program and in a local rehabilitation center with an Alzheimer unit. The staff of the local Alzheimer's facility planted gardens with and for the patients. As for the question of how to keep the patients from eating the flowers, the staff researched which species planted were possibly poisonous. At least, the two apple trees are not only surviving but producing!

Building the Karmapa's Peace Garden.

Traditionally, gardens have been a literal lifeline for some Native American tribes. On the wind-blown grasslands of South Dakota, members of the Lakota (Sioux) tribe live on reservations in pockets of government housing. Since there is very little wood for heat, their houses depend on electricity or propane. Yet, if people do not have jobs, cannot pay bills, some freeze to death. In 1997, it was so cold (-70°) and distressful that some of the young people, already overwhelmed by cold, hunger, lack of purpose or hope, took their own lives.

Once a powerful people who hunted buffalo and gathered berries, nuts and tubers as staples which they traded for other necessities, the Lakota are now almost totally dependent on government commodities for food and are often reduced to despair. However, Jacques Seronde, my son, knows what some courageous people are doing to help alleviate these prevailing conditions:

Despite such widespread hopelessness, a group of individuals organized themselves as the Wilconzani Club—"healthful in body and spirit"—with the express purpose of restoring beauty to their lives and strengthening their connections to the many beings of our Mother Earth. In 1996, working with Ann Krush, agriculture instructor at the State Gleska University (SGU) on the Rosebud Reservation, they established the Garden for Health program.

To see the earth as it truly is, small and blue in that eternal silence where it floats, is to see riders on the earth together, brothers on that bright loveliness in the eternal cold—brothers who know now they are truly brothers.
ARCHIBALD MACLEISH

Community outreach coordinators were hired to help families create their gardens. They also provided technical assistance throughout the growing season, helped with food storage and preservation activities and offered nutritional guidance for the prevention of widespread diabetes.

Ann Krush, for one, taught by engaging her class in active doing. Her students were mostly women in their forties with grown families, with time to attend her class. Together, they grew seedlings under grow lights; dug mulch into small demonstration beds; planted traditional squash, beans, corn and tomatoes, as well as trees, plum and chokecherry—willow and lilac—whatever would grow in that land of sand and ever-blowing wind in the South Dakota wilderness.

Faster and faster, family gardens spread across the reservation. A farmers market has opened, also a permaculture course was offered by a Navajo teacher, who told the children how local plants can provide food, dyes, medicines and hope.

In the gardens, GfH has added some form of visual art—a mosaic or mural, a wall, benches, water features, a walkway of stone mosaics or a sculpture built with local materials. GfH also encouraged dancing, musical events, meetings and poetry readings.

Of all the projects GfH created or enlarged, the one involving elementary school children was the most rewarding. Enthusiastic to try new adventures, most children quickly reveled in getting dirty, transforming mud pies into depressions for new seeds, patting and watering them. Finally, with time, they could joyfully observe stems, leaves, flowers and fruits appearing. Together, they had learned to enjoy the varying textures of soil—rough with granite pebbles or slick with clay or slippery cinders. They could smell the fragrance of the earth after watering or during a welcome rain. After mixing soil and grasses, hay, leaves and kitchen vegetable scrapings with wood chips and manure, they could make compost—that delicious feast for plants. And what were those crawling creatures? Worms, snails? Or flying bugs with brightly-colored wings or shiny bodies? What insects protect the leaves? Ladybugs? And which ones did they have to pick off roses or beans?

Most interesting of all was what the children themselves could eat: lettuce and squash buds, beet

The Earth is our mother. She nourishes us. And that which we put into the ground, she returns to us.
BIG THUNDER,
ALGONQUIAN TRIBE

leaves, spinach and those sweet orange roots, carrots!

What was learned over those years of trying to fill some obvious, but un-acknowledged, gaps in these children's education? Did we give sufficient encour-agement to overburdened teachers who loved gardens but had little time to teach children about working with the soil? We wondered if these children knew—in their hearts and hands and minds—that all of us in the world depend on the gardens of the Earth for our lives. Perhaps, some of these seeds germinated and grew in their hearts.

The challenge of reeducation facing schools today is to urge people of all ages to recognize what is at stake: the Earth itself, its life forms, even the ability to live and breathe. Revolutionary thinking is needed in schools to combat boredom and frustration, to stimulate physical and mental activity for students, to create incentives and time for them to grow without being pressed about future jobs. Teachers must be allowed time to teach, to excite students with opportunities other than computers, disruptive behavior, or iPods!

There is a garden in every childhood, an enchanted place where colors are brighter, the air softer, and the morning more fragrant than ever again.

Elizabeth Lawrence

Teachers, also, need time to imagine, to be trained in new ways, to be able to prepare alternate lessons for new adventures. Field trips allow children to see, feel, hear and smell the world of nature as meadows, forests, ponds and waterways. This revolution is about healing children suffering from hyperactivity, low attention span and junk foods—and about other ways of earning self-pride and confidence.

The overriding consideration for teaching in schools should be the Earth: its conservation, its characteristics and bio-diversity—its luminous presence and beauty. Undoubtedly, the Earth being central to our lives, every school curriculum is going to require new sensitivity, new training, new knowledge, enthusiasm and energy. By relating nature to every subject taught in schools—history, social studies, sciences, arts, and others—we can begin to understand its opportunities and its marvels. We can, also, become more aware of the ecological crises we face because of our contradictory policies regarding the economics of food, fuel and fertilizers, water and climate change.

Today, Gardens for Humanity has a new direction and energy. Newly planned programs are taking advantage of the many opportunities being offered. Instead of building gardens for groups or institutions, GfH works with clients who truly want to work. Clients need to demonstrate the desire to learn every step in fashioning a garden—from

Adele and the children of Sedona's Terra Rosa School creating a stone mosaic.

143

The care of the Earth is our most ancient and most worthy, and after all our most pleasing responsibility. To cherish what remains of it and to foster its renewal is our only hope.

WENDELL BERRY

making soil to planting, harvesting and maintaining it. The idea is: Don't catch fish and give it to the people. Train people to catch fish.

GfH is part of an Agricultural Renaissance in Arizona's Verde Valley, created by Diane Dearmore. From those interested in this Renaissance a new board of enthusiastic, trained green leaders is emerging. Members from local community-supported farms, community food banks, gardeners, farmers markets, teachers from local schools and colleges and interested lay people share ideas and teach important workshops.

GfH's dream is to work with Arizona's Verde Valley community to utilize sustainable resources and be willing and able to help its members. Help includes learning to use available technical means of harvesting wind, sun, waves and biomass for our fuels and home-grown produce for our foods and medicines. The immediate step is to expand home gardening into the vision of small working farms, ideally as in the bountiful community-supported agriculture (CSA's) farms. These are prototypes showing that successful farming is an art.

Just as great art requires that observation, knowledge, skill and determination are needed, and just as art is motivated by intense passion, so too is farming an art in the hands of a true farmer. The farmer, as artist, watches and implements every detail of preparing, planting, growing and harvesting. With added composted manure, he gives back to the earth what he has taken from it in his annual completion of the year's cycle. Under nurturing care the land blooms and the farmer takes pride in the quality of his work.

The farmer's small farm is not an industrial monolith, owned by some corporate agribusiness, inspired by greed for ever-increasing profits. The small farmer's method of preparation (by hand, by horse-plough, by small tractor or rototiller) does not employ huge machines. Seeds on this farm are not genetically altered to be sterile, never to reproduce, and necessitating new purchase each year—thanks to ambitions of certain industries to monopolize the sources of food in a hungry world.

What small farmers desire is their own land, rich in nutrients that have not been leached out by over-fertilization and over-production. Water sources will stop being poisoned by pesticides and herbicides; natural antidotes for garden pests will be used. These farmers will be working with nature, using their animals' manure and hay from fields, as well as kitchen leavings and green vegetable parings, to make compost. Fruit trees and berries will support them and their families and will also contribute to

A few things to remember when planting a garden:

- Gardens require ongoing nurturing and love. Ideally, they need maintenance on a daily basis.
- Each garden needs a passionate person who observes, knows or learns what makes every plant bloom. Such a person should be in charge of this care. Even a small payment could help make this a permanent, ongoing job.
- Every child deserves a caring, knowledgeable teacher who inspires, not only to learn, but also to show others what is being learned.
- These processes of physically creating gardens, as well as expressing feelings through the arts, are forms of healing, of literally grounding overly tense destructive children and adults.
- That art, in its diverse expressions, is a way of defining and sharing the incredible beauty of the world.

Hopis in garden with Diane Dearmore

the local community, grocery and farmers markets.

The art of small farming lies in its conception of wholeness, of completeness, of balance. Newly educated farmers need to take care of each step: planting a diversity of crops to nurture people, animals and burgeoning wildlife; balancing use of the land through crop rotation; and developing a symbiotic relationship with streams, meadows, forests and other human beings. Part of the training is to learn to care for domestic animals, each one a separate living being; how to kill for food humanely and utilize all parts of the meat; and how to can, freeze and dry vegetables.

Some communities that invest in their farmers provide an advance payment in the springtime in exchange for a regular percentage of every crop grown throughout the year. If there is bad weather and a resulting small crop, the community client still receives his/her portion, and the farmer is saved from financial disaster. (Too many small farms have lost their mortgages or been absorbed by agribusiness because of no financial insurance.) Community-supported agriculture (CSA) often obtains and restores agrarian lands where little farms used to thrive. An agricultural renaissance is needed to bring local food back into communities, into the supermarkets and also into the farmers markets and food banks. This fresh food can be offered to the hungry and homeless in our towns and cities, as well as to school children, hospital patients, seniors and local restaurant diners. It can be used to combat diabetes and to prevent the pervasive ill-health and obesity of many adults and children. Locally grown food introduces delicious taste, inspires new ways of preparing and caring, and creates opportunities for children to learn how to grow and prepare nutritious meals.

Perhaps, this is what President Obama has asked of us: to be more self-sufficient, to develop pride in helping ourselves and serving others, to be able to share knowledge in building communities with pride in achievement. He wants Americans to participate in the process of doing each job properly. Obama's own values are spelled out in his books: his ways of sharing; his enormous energy; his passion to bring the these values, their inner truths, into every heart.

Americans, for their part, have enormous new opportunities to contribute, to create self-sustaining communities, to re-envision educational systems, to learn how to think clearly—without fear—about how to change, to literally shape the means of survival for ourselves and our children.

Coming to grips with the following truths has now become imperative for our survival:

Burn down your cities and leave our farms, and your cities will spring up again as if by magic; but destroy our farms and the grass will grow in the streets of every city in the country.
WILLIAM JENNINGS BRYAN

Member of Hopi tribe picking corn

■ Human beings (as well as other living species) are ultimately dependent on plants for oxygen, for food and for the base of most medicines, clothing and shelter. Without caring for and preserving them, human beings are not long for the world.

■ Nature is our greatest teacher, to be observed and listened to, beloved, not exploited and destroyed. Every living creature, every mineral, each diverse part of the biosphere, the universe, has its own unique use, its way of contributing, its interrelationship with every other part. Our world is numinous. God is creator and part of it, and within us. It is our Sacred Garden.

■ Gardens of beauty can be cultivated within each human being and the love planted there can be transferred—with hard work and patience—into every patch of soil.

Can microcosms of our Sacred Garden spring up everywhere? It depends on us!

ASPEN ON PILGRIMAGE

Voices of the Future

PART IV

Ultimately, the decision to save the environment must come from the human heart. The key point is a call for a genuine sense of universal responsibility that is based on love, compassion and clear awareness.

H.H. The Dalai Lama

CHAPTER THIRTEEN

Visionary Voices

Stars will burn through the sheets of the clouds
and a new voice is heard — Life is a river, Time is a river,
Love is a river — will that voice be our own?
Now Mr. Drought shadows us — a monster spreading fear.
The stars will burn through the sheets of the clouds
and a new voice must be born — that of our own.

- Excerpt from "The Great Houdini" by James Bishop, Jr.

New voices of hope and encouragement from the Earth are speaking to us. They say that the garden that is the blooming spirit within us feels new energies, arousing our sensibilities through the arts and metaphysics, and by being in nature. These powerful energies reach out as old voices speak as new. When people listen, they know that these are their linkages—bridges to God and to the forces of life.

At the same time, physicists and metaphysicians are starting to understand that they are sharing the same universe. The cutting-edge field of quantum physics now clearly demonstrates that science and spirituality embrace this world, with its vast areas of the known, unknown and undiscovered dimensions, in a dialogue of mutual excitement. Science had to evolve to its present level in order to establish that, historically, these two approaches deal with the same cosmic reality, but from different perspectives.

Each supports a centralizing "cause" of life, an underlying meaning of initial importance. It appears as if the most celebrated discipline of our age—physics—and a misunderstood area of contemporary thought—mysticism—are extending the realms of human imagination and spiritual searching. And, at last, they stand in accord.

The task of transforming and redeeming the Earth will require the enlightened imagination of the visionary in all of us. This is the primary voice that we all must hear. Its magic invites us into the imagery of the Garden of Eden in the Bible and into the poetry of creation in the Koran, mandalas and spiritual texts of the world.

The dream of the Dalai Lama—that Tibet might become a world oasis, a park, a Shangri-La, turning the mythical Shambhala into a magical reality—is one example. In the face of present Chinese aggression, this seems like a pipe-dream, but it is a vision, the true voice of the future. The Shambhala can be considered a symbol of the whole Earth as a spiritual garden, a place of endowment. To better understand this concept of the Shambhala, it is important to see how it is intertwined in the lives of current Tibetan leaders. In Tibetan tradition, a Karmapa is a twin-soul to a Dalai Lama: a spiritual as opposed to a political force. "Like the Dalai Lama, the Karmapa is regarded as an embodiment of compassion. The sole purpose of the Karmapa's incarnation is to lead living beings from the suffering of samsara into freedom—the realization of mind's deepest pure nature. . ." (from *Music in the Sky, The Life, Art and Teachings of the 17th Karmapa*, by Michele Martin, Snow Lion Publishers).

The present 17th Karmapa, His Holiness Gwalwa Karmapa Ogyen Trinley Dorje, again within traditional Tibetan belief, is the reincarnated soul of the 16th Karmapa, who died in 1981. In fact, this boy, who celebrated his twenty-first birthday on June 26, 2006, was held hostage in Tibet for his whole life. The Chinese know the power of his symbolic mission in the land where they are committing genocide. In 1999, on the eve of the new century, he escaped with six other lamas, risking death by the elements rather than spiritual and, perhaps, literal death by the Chinese. It is rumored that they chose the worst winter storm to cover their carefully planned escape, by walking, driving by Jeep, undetected, over mountain passes, then by Jeep again to where a helicopter could bring them to Nepal. Arriving five days later in India, they immediately went to the Dalai Lama.

Today, having been recognized by the Dalai Lama as the true Karmapa, Ogyen Trinley Dorje teaches in India and visits America. To complement his vision of world peace—in recognition that life on Earth itself is at risk—he has now expanded his teaching into a mission to save our planet.

The Karmapa knows that the existing tasks of healing ourselves, our communities and our whole Earth remain formidable. The challenges of the future are enormous—even more so now that we are at the edge of cyberspace, genetic engineering and robotic technology.

And, meanwhile, as if in encouragement to all of us who are confronting these challenges, strange new crop circles have appeared all over the world. They may not be new at all except in our recent discovery of them; they may well have existed in the folklore of many cultures as "fairy rings."

These crop circles are most frequently observed among the fields of wheat or barley in England's West Country, the Salisbury Plain and Wiltshire, Somerset and Dorset. They also appear in other parts of Europe and America. Although a few circles have been exposed as

His Holiness, the 17th Gyalwang Karmapa, Ogyen Trinley Dorje as a young boy (above) and in a recent photo.

World, we live and die on your lap. On you we play out all our woes and joys. You are our home, old ancient one. Forever we cherish you; we could not bear your loss. We wish to transform you into the pure realm of our dreams, into a field where all creatures live without prejudice, all equal. Our wish to embrace you is unchangeably steadfast. To that end be the ground which sustains us all.

H.H. THE 17TH KARMAPA

deliberate hoaxes, even those human circle-makers often claim to have been inspired by aliens, or have felt strange energies, and "seen" symbols and glyphs as they were making them. However, these crop circle phenomena are unique; most people think they are made by unknown forces or extraterrestrials. They appear overnight without harming or changing the grain itself. Often covering large fields, they are most clearly seen from airplanes.

What are the messages of the crop circles? Each one seems to embody some extraordinary design of radiant beauty, which quickens in us a response of pure wonder and awe, an intrinsic means of healing. Is this a supernatural force creating a mystical language of the eye so that we wonder who is speaking to us—angels or aliens in disguise? Are they enticements to discover our innermost reverence? Or are they warnings to make us listen to the voices of the universe before it is too late?

One of the most poignant and eloquent answering voices of the 20th century, one which speaks of the luminous beauty of the Earth and its mystical relationship with the universe, belongs to the late Father Thomas Berry. Almost alone among Christian churches' spokesmen, Father Berry's writings warn about our increasing destruction of the Earth and isolation from nature. He said that our conviction that human beings are a dominant and superior species lies at the heart of Western civilization beliefs and actions.[1] To combat this conviction, Father Berry devoted his life, through his many books, lectures and courses, to the offering of spiritual reeducation to our whole society. He teaches the dimensions of a "New Story" to be learned, the "New Work" to be accomplished.

In this ecological age, Father Berry says:

What we need, what we are ultimately groping toward, is the sensitivity required to understand and respond to the psychic energies deep in the very structure of reality itself. Our knowledge and control of the environment is not absolute knowledge or absolute control. It is a cooperative understanding and response to forces that will bring about a proper unfolding of the earth process if we do not ourselves obstruct or distort these forces that seek their proper expression.[2]

Many people hope and believe that the meaning of his great dream is that we, mankind, will come of age, will become mature enough to be cooperative and be able to absorb Earth's luminous presence into our consciousness.

These prophetic voices, which we honor in our great visionaries, are recumbent in all of us, just waiting to be inspired to think and to act! These are the people who are showing us the way.

There is a vitality, a life force, an energy, a quickening that is translated through you into action and because there is only one of you in all of time this expression is unique. And if you block it, it will never exist through any other medium and be lost.

MARTHA GRAHAM

---

[1] The Rev. Fr. Thomas Berry, C.P. was an extraordinary Catholic priest of the Passionist order, a cosmologist, cultural historian and eco-theologian. He is world famous for advocating deep ecology and eco-spirituality, for proposing that a deep understanding of the history and functioning of the evolving universe is a necessary inspiration and guide for our own effective functioning as individuals and as a species. Five of his eight books are classics in the field of leading cosmological and environmental thought.
[2] *The Dream of the Earth,* Thomas Berry, Sierra Club Books, 1988

CHAPTER FOURTEEN

How People Are Meeting the Challenge

The time for action is passing. The devastation increases.
The time is limited. The Great Work remains to be done. This is
not a situation that can be remedied by trivial or painless means.
A largeness of vision and a supreme dedication are needed.

- Thomas Berry

P rescient green thinkers and designers are everywhere around us. Among them are Al Gore; architect Bill McDonough; writers Thomas Berry, Joanna Macy, Bill McKibben, Wendell Berry, Lester Brown and Amory Lovins; poet-naturalists Loren Eiseley and Gary Snyder; essayist Barry Lopez and many other activists. Together, they visualize and advocate sustainable communities, indeed a more sustainable world, that will cope with our environmental challenges. They are answering questions such as these:

- What must we do to increase our love and respect for the Earth?

- How do we enter into a spiritual relationship with nature?

- How do we create more sustainable food production?

- How can we protect the biodiversity of seeds from gene tampering by corporations?

- How do we replant habitats of forests and marshes and sea nurseries of eelgrass for clams and mussels?

- How do we transform factory farms into more humane quarters for domesticated animals?

- How do we construct new green buildings insulated to withstand a variety of temperatures from 120°F to -90°F as well as other climatic abnormalities?
- How do we communicate with each other honestly, allowing time and space for debate and questioning?

* * * * *

Beginning at the deepest level of our lives, people are already transforming their consciousness to become aware of the soul's power. Writer and teacher V. Vernon Woolf, Ph.D., offers a bridge between physics and metaphysics as a way of expanding inner consciousness of more people. As a physicist, he demonstrates a way to see the world in holographic form, as an integrated whole of knowledge and existence, mind and heart. He has devised a method of absorbing and teaching information from all sources, of viewing life through an expanded framework he calls holodynamics. His method of transforming consciousness is through a holographic model of thinking that hears and uses all dimensions of reality, including hyperspace parapsychological energies and extrasensory intuitions.

Dr. Woolf's major message urges people to expand their sensitivities to reach their fullest potential—aware of the soul in all living creatures, so that they choose the most creative solutions to present and future challenges.

To learn how to survive in coming emergencies, Dr. Woolf teaches intensive courses in holodynamics, training teams of teachers and offering methods of expanded thinking and healing. Perhaps, when enough people are awakened, world consciousness can be transformed and people will have the determination and the strength to save and heal the planet!

My soul can find no staircase to heaven unless it be through earth's loveliness.
MICHELANGELO

* * * * *

The natural world is the larger sacred community to which we belong. To be alienated from this community is to become destitute in all that makes us human. To damage this community is to diminish our own existence.

THOMAS BERRY

The Japanese researcher Masaru Emoto, Ph.D., records collecting and freezing samples of water from many sources, both pure and polluted. By cutting cross-sections of these specimens and photographing their crystalline images, he claims that pure water evokes radiant snowflake-shaped images, while polluted samples distort these images into horrifying shapes! Furthermore, according to Dr. Emoto, when water samples were exposed to words like love, gratitude and peace, their physical formation (after being frozen again and photographed) was transformed to become more beautiful. Conversely, he reported that talking to the water in harsh or degrading terms turned their molecular crystalline forms into distorted and disfigured shapes! Since at least 80 percent of human physical cell formations are comprised of water, some believe that what we think—what we project through the water of our innermost atoms—has huge ramifications.

Another example of change on a global scale lies in Japan's commitment to recycling. That ancient country is recycling on both individual and national levels, partly inspired by dangerous health issues attributable to industrialization, but also by the urgent need for an energy-efficient and environmentally cleaner economy. Everything from bottle caps and roadside trash, to cell phones, watches and automobiles is collected and broken down to separate their component metals and reused. Even the wasted earth, from mines after coal or gold ore is extracted, is examined for valuables; a ton may yield five grams of gold; a cell phone may give 400 grams; enough old cell phones of recovered gold may eventually be formed into a gold brick worth about $76,000.00!

The goal of Japanese citizens (and their towns) is to be sustainable; everything they use can be re-used. If not, then they believe it should not be produced. People save everything, including chopsticks, carrying-bags and paper; even garbage becomes valuable by sorting its contents and creating new products. Energy can be saved by using biomass burners instead of oil. Grass mats on roofs can reduce heat; solar panels on roofs can produce electricity. Plants (especially trees) are used everywhere to reduce heat and to beautify. Even the red roadside flowers were genetically engineered and planted to absorb noxious emissions from cars and to help evaporate runoff.

The automobile, a major cause of global pollution, is undergoing change. Hybrid cars produced by Toyota and Honda use more electricity and less gasoline to power their engines, reduce emissions and increase mileage. Toyota has also revolutionized the Prius factory, which now relies on hybrid power, drawing 50 percent of its electricity from solar panels and 50 percent from capturing waste heat generated within the plant. The facility has reduced its carbon dioxide emissions to half of what they were in 1990, despite an increase in production. It eliminated production of landfill waste in 1999 and dispensed with incinerated waste a few months later.

Why hasn't America launched such an urgent program?

* * * * *

In Denmark, meanwhile, the inhabitants (mostly farmers) on the island of Samso, have changed their living habits dramatically over the past ten years. Instead of being dependent on oil and coal, they now rely on renewable energies. Solar panels are installed on roofs and in fields to heat houses and water. Wind turbines of many sizes abound, with small ones on individual roofs, large banks of turbines offshore and in fields to produce electricity. Some farmers grow rapeseed to produce oil to run their tractors. Others use straw, which is brought to special factory plants where it is burnt for heating water, which is then pumped through underground pipes

Compressed aluminum cans prepared for recycling.

Wind turbines on the Island of Samso.

to homes for both hot water and heat. Samso is now able to provide the electricity for all its citizens, and its wind turbines produce enough electricity for much of mainland Denmark.

How was this community of ordinary people—not university intellectuals or scientists—persuaded to make these changes? It was not easy. They did not have corporate or government funds. But they did obtain one particular government-offered financial incentive for the most convincing plan to cut carbon outputs and boost renewable energy generation. Samso won the competition.

But the real job of coaxing conservative islanders to make this plan work was put into the hands of a local environmental studies teacher. He went to every village meeting, talked to groups and individuals, answered questions and encouraged ideas. However, the impetus to get action was not fear of climate change or threat of ozone or global warming. Action came from the citizens of Samso who wanted to involve themselves in something that could make a difference in the world.

Instead of accepting funding from Shell Oil Company to build their wind turbines—Shell's terms of owning the turbines were too high—Samso citizens decided to own their own constructed work. They formed a company, took shares in the first turbines and in their own future. Some of the initial money was then contributed by their government, the European Union, and by local businesses, but most of it came out of their own pockets. They had determined that they wanted to change how they used energy without harming the planet and without giving up the good life.

In a matter of ten years, all the initial costs were repaid by the sale of electricity generated, enough to service all Samso's citizens and export markets. Samso Island is another example of the worldwide shift

164

of paradigms toward sustainability. Their carbon footprint of released carbon dioxide has been cut back 140 percent, and the oil and coal burning plants that once serviced Samso have been dismantled.

* * * * *

Back in the U.S. a new visionary community of green rebuilding was created after a horrendous tornado in 2007 devastated the town of Greensburg, Kansas, according to the *New York Times.*

In Greensburg, Mike Estes manages one of four new "Leadership in Energy and Environmental Design" (LEED) certified buildings. It is a John Deere dealership that is "energy-efficient, wind-powered, water-conserving and environmentally sensitive." He said: "Two years ago, the whole town needed to be rebuilt. And we needed industry. We are learning that green makes sense."

By earning a United States Green Building Council's LEED gold-platinum award, Greensburg met formidable standards for a "truly sustainable community that balances economic, ecological and social aspects of development." After the tornado, the city leaders chose a new goal: "to build a sense of economic dynamism that would generate new businesses and jobs, and would persuade Greensburg's talented young people not to leave." In so many words, the city's citizens said, "What do you do when you start with a clean slate? You want to build it better. Right?"

So, at Mike Estes' dealership, they learned how to design features such as skylights and electrical systems which cut energy use by half, use plumbing features that save almost 40,000 gallons of water a year and employ two wind turbines that spin in a steady wind and generate part of the dealership's electricity.

In Greensburg, other features either being considered or actively built include:

- ■ a laboratory for research on sustainable design and community development,
- ■ an ordinance that all municipal buildings larger than 4,000 square feet be built to LEED-platinum standards.

Out of clutter ...
find simplicity.
From discord . . .
find harmony.
In the middle
of difficulty
lies opportunity.
ALBERT EINSTEIN

- a city-owned 10,000 square-foot three to four million dollar business incubator that offers temporary space at low rent for ten small businesses and that is financed by a combination of private and corporate funds and the U.S. Department of Agriculture.
- a renovated courthouse that includes: highly insulated walls, geothermal pumps for heating and cooling, high-performance lighting and controls and other environmental and clean energy features that qualify for LEED-gold designations.
- a new hospital that incorporates natural light; high-performance insulating glass; light-sensing dimmers; motion sensors; an on-site wind turbine to generate electricity; a biological filtration system to process all waste-water from the laundry, showers and lavatories; and a system to capture rainwater to flush toilets.

And Greensburg's principle showcase is:

- a new LEED-certified townhouse complex of 200 new homes, comprising 40,000 square feet, built at a cost of four million dollars, and many built with energy efficiency, water conservation and other environmental values in mind.

With all these energy-saving innovations in a state that consistently ranks among the top ten in oil and natural gas production, the higher initial installation costs have been more than offset by significantly lower operating costs. Mike Estes says that he is "saving the equivalent of $25,000-$30,000 annually in energy and water costs compared with the old building."

Courageous Kansas citizens speak to all of us who may be in mortgaged homes, in collapsing businesses or in despair: People saw that a terrible tragedy could be made into something valuable and durable and better. Look what we can do when we think about this in a new way.

* * * * *

Throughout the world people are demanding action to combat climate change. This is what Andres R. Edwards calls *The Sustainability Revolution*, which is also the title of his book in which he writes: "Like the Industrial Revolution, it is far-reaching and having a profound impact, shaping everything from the places we live and work to the foods we eat and the endeavors we pursue as individuals and communities."[1]

David W. Orr, in his foreword to *The Sustainability Revolution*, says:

It is happening first at the periphery of power and wealth, where revolutions often start. It is evident: in farmers beginning to mimic natural systems in order to preserve their soil and land . . . in a new attitude emerging everywhere about the values of biological diversity and species protection . . . in the rapid development of technologies that harness sunlight and wind . . . in the burgeoning interest in green building, green architecture, green engineering and green communities.

This powerful new paradigm is evident in thinking and technology of a growing number of businesses selling "products of service."[2] According to Orr:

. . . preserving natural capital [is] a matter of conscience and profit . . . in a new religious sensibility across the full spectrum of faith traditions that regards stewardship of the Earth as obligatory . . . it is evident in education and the emergence of new ways to think about the human role in nature that stretch our perspective to whole systems and out to the far horizons of imagination.

According to Edwards, this new sustainability revolution has already become larger in its implications than the Industrial Revolution. It is worldwide and multicultural. In fact, at this writing

The closer we get to a virtuous circle, in which our work, our home life, our ethics and our spirituality are mutually reinforcing, the closer we will be to achieving genuine sustainability

JAMES WILSDON,
FORUM FOR THE FUTURE

---

[1] *The Sustainability Revolution*, Andres R. Edwards, New Society Publishers, 2005
[2] Products of service are locallly grown foods, locally produced energies.

Whatever befalls the earth, befalls the people of the earth. Man did not weave the web of life; he is merely a strand in it.

CHIEF SEATTLE

in 2010, it is finally prodding our American corporations, local chambers of commerce, and the media into paying attention to climate change, to the ozone layer and to species which are disappearing forever. Its very core can be visualized as a triangle supporting the Three E's: Ecology/Environment, Economy/Employment, and Equity/Equality.

To be sustainable, a world in balance must be imagined and created—each of these E's is equally

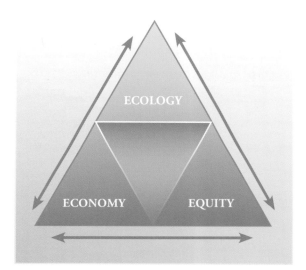

important and dependent on one another to function properly. Each has legitimate needs that must be respected by the other two. For instance, it is not enough to stop the world's lumber or food companies from destroying global rainforests—people must find compensations for the companies and the communities and creative ways to expand economies on which the communities depend.

According to Edwards, corporate owners should respect the power of nature to allow resources of trees, vegetables, animals, fish and other denizens of the seas to recover. Both companies and environmentalists should recognize the rights of the communities in which they work—both human and animal. Ideally the men and women involved should have an equal share of the profits of a healthy economy and also have respect for the natural inhabitants of the rainforests, oceans and farmlands.

In *The Sustainability Revolution,* Edwards provides detailed analysis to implement these criteria for the successful practice of the Three E's. He also lists hundreds of examples and the names of a growing number of imaginative and ingenious companies and groups that are taking positive actions. To implement these Three E's, he adds a fourth E: Education.

Furthermore, America's educational system should adopt and expand the criteria for sustainable principles initiated in the Stockholm Conference (1972) and the Earth Summit (1987). These culminated, writes Edwards, in the United Nations Conference on Environment and Development and created the Earth Charter, which "strives to reconcile the twin requirements of a high quality environment and a healthy economy for all people of the world, while identifying key areas of responsibility as well as offering preliminary cost estimates for success." Progress toward that goal has been mixed.

Plans to protect air and water, wilderness and wildlife are, in fact, plans to protect man.
STEWART UDALL

* * * * *

Another antidote for industrial exploitation lies in an extraordinary vision for our future: that of Mohammed Yunus, a former professor who was teaching in Bangladesh. So appalled was he by the extreme poverty of some of his neighbors that he sought help for them from local banks. All the banks lacked confidence in the capacities of the local people to repay their loans. So, Yunus decided to fund a small program giving small loans to a few women: enough for a few chickens, an ox to help plow a garden, sheep to produce wool; tools for gardening, or perhaps, a loom or a spinning wheel; or seeds for food or hemp to make rope. His action was based on his trust that an initial helping hand would generate enough capital to realize a small dream. His foresight and generous hand were repaid a thousand-fold. Each woman was able to repay him and to share her profit and persuade other neighbors to follow their dreams.

At first, Yunus's confidence was offered almost exclusively to women. Women, he knew, would work with all their might to help their families survive. As the program grew, men became involved. Soon his idea spread throughout the world. Receiving a Nobel Prize for Peace in 2006, he insisted on sharing his honors with some of the recipients of early grants, who were by then better off.

In today's collapsing Tower-of-Babel world of bankers, the small voice of Mohammed Yunus has become like a trumpet blast! It has a piercing clarity that can echo into the darkest caverns of poverty and hopelessness everywhere!

Slow Food—Slow Money

A fascinating new approach to help small business and entrepreneurs reach out to enlighten their communities is being offered by the American financier Woody Tasch. As a former Chairman of Investors' Circle, he has been dismayed by the way American capital (and everyman's money) is leaving our towns and cities and country at ever-increasing speed as if, as it "circulates the globe, money is sucking oxygen out of the air, fertility out of the soil and culture out of local communities."

In attempting to offset this outflow of literally trillions of dollars he has initiated a social investment organization called the Slow Money Alliance. His idea is inspiring donations from donors for seed capital[3] in order to build "local capacity to invest in local food systems." Further, he says: "The task at hand now is to build a whole new kind of economy that is restorative, meaning that as jobs and welfare are created, we are also healing broken social and environmental systems. And SLOW MONEY is a step toward the first principles of a deeper version of social investing."

This idea and term are analogous to an earlier concept which was developed in recent years: SLOW FOOD. From Italy, and now spiraling out through Europe and to America, the concept of Slow Food was developed by Italians who appreciate good food as a direct antithesis to American fast food. They advocate that vegetables and animals must be raised with careful nurturing in adherence to their quality. Food must be prepared by hand and cooked with patience for whatever time is necessary (no microwaves), then eaten slowly to savor their delicious aromas and tastes—with pleasure.

So the term "Slow Food" has direct relation to our need to return to old-fashioned means of farming with patience and care—within new contexts.

Our world has enough for each person's need, but not for his greed.
MAHATMA GANDHI

---

[3] *Acres USA,* November 2009, "Bringing Money Back to Earth," an interview with Woody Tasch, pp. 52-61.

170

Tasch explains:

We are talking about entrepreneurship, including farmers. We want to give these entrepreneurs the capital they need to grow their small food enterprise . . . We're introducing the concept of place. By place, I mean not only the community, not only the region in which we live, but all the way down to the soil. We want to put organic matter back into the soil, we want the carbons back in the soil. We want to preserve soil fertility. At a slightly larger level we want to restore and preserve the fertility of our communities—the social fertility, the health of our communities and our bio-regions. We want to invest closer to home, and we want to know what we're investing in. If you connect these two things, you can see that it's a much more radical, in the true source of the term, approach to investing.

Apart from Slow Money there is another means of raising capital, such as, a green mini-credit bank—a combination of Mohammed Yunus's Grameen Banks and Slow Money. Yunus's bank is being used in America now, but only at the very deepest levels of poverty, mostly urban.

It seems that a green bank could support all the factors in a healthy agricultural community. The truth is there is need for seed money to train future farmers; money is needed to buy tools and livestock, to teach about irrigation and restoring land. Also needed is salary money for teachers of natural history and husbandry.

* * * * *

Two of the most compelling voices of the future can be found in the combined work of architect William McDonough and his partner, German biochemist Michael Braungart. In their environmental masterpiece, *Cradle to Cradle,* they write that, "We see a world of abundance, not limits. In the midst of a great deal of talk about reducing the human ecological footprint, we offer a different vision. What if humans designed products and systems that celebrate an abundance of human creativity, culture and productivity? That are so intelligent and safe, our species leaves an ecological footprint to delight in, not lament?"

To realize such a future, according to *Cradle to Cradle,* it is not just a matter of cleaning up existing messes and recycling wastes under present conditions (in themselves huge challenges). Rather, it is an urgent call to examine what we do: what we eat, what we produce, how we live and what effects we are having on the Earth. It is not just a question of recycling. "Recycling is an aspirin, alleviating a rather large collective hangover . . . overconsumption. The simple truth is that all of our major environmental concerns are either caused, or contributed to, by the ever-increasing consumption of goods and services."[4]

For their part, McDonough and Braungart advocate, as an initial step, the four R's: Reduce, Reuse, Recycle and Regulate. All of these verbs lead to a saving of money, to less pollution and waste, to Eco-Efficiency.

They also call for an economic system which is not as dependent upon consumption. With a little self-discipline people can learn not to want so much "stuff" and not to order it. They need to find out how to reuse what they can. However, if not supervised, reuse of materials can lead to abuses such as reusing sewage sludge by putting it into animal feed, or storing dangerous toxins in containers which

I truly believe that we in this generation must come to terms with nature, and I think we're challenged, as mankind has never been challenged before, to prove our maturity and our mastery, not of nature but of ourselves.

RACHEL CARSON

---

[4] William Rathje's 1998 book: *Use Less Stuff: Environmental Solutions for Who We Really Are*

eventually corrode, or releasing them into the air, the ocean or the soil. However, regulations, too, can inhibit progress, and too many can inhibit actions for reform.

In fact, according to McDonough and Braungart, as they developed their ideas further, the aspiration of eco-efficiency is not as beneficial as its namers had hoped because it does not go deep enough. It makes an older, destructive system seem less so, like putting a Band-Aid on a festering wound. The real question, they feel, is one of redesigning, of proper planning and of using materials that are safe and reusable. Materials can be categorized as biodegradable or toxic and, with proper management, can be separated and cleansed. Then, products, even poisons, can be retrieved so that they cannot harm humans and wildlife.

Architect McDonough insists that, "We now have eco-efficient buildings which actually are not. They use:

1) energy-saving seals for leaks and windows

2) dark-tinted glass (both 1 and 2 contributing to dark, windowless rooms, and sometimes claustrophobia)

3) fossil fuels—from power plants—to save money."

McDonough continues, instead, "Look at the way nature reacts and recycles—a cherry tree, for example.

A cherry tree:

1) provides food for animals, insects, microorganisms, as fruit, leaves, blossoms, and rotting trunk branches

2) enriches ecosystem, sequesters carbon, produces oxygen

3) cleanses air and water."

McDonough concludes that: "What we need are buildings redesigned like a cherry tree. Following nature's master design with:

Only after the last tree has been cut down. Only after the last river has been poisoned. Only after the last fish has been caught. Only then will you find that money cannot be eaten.
CREE INDIAN PROPHECY

1)   Light and air pouring in through windows and skylights—no dark glass

2)   Layer of grasses on roofs which

   a) attract birds

   b) absorb water run-off

   c) protects roofs from thermal shock and ultraviolet degradation

   d) provide insulation from heat in summer, cold in winter

3)   If made of wood, can be reused as firewood or for rebuilding."

Such a green building is attractive to its occupants and its work force. McDonough and Braungart use this design in all of their new green work because it reduces the expense incurred by losing workers because of poor working conditions and cost of recruiting, employing and retaining new ones.

Using this model for even more ambitious rebuilding, McDonough and Braungart helped the present-day chairman of Ford Motor Company, William Clay Ford, Jr., transform the aging, monolithic factory his great grandfather named the River Rouge. While his great-grandfather's vision of creating manufacturing plants included powerhouses, body shops, assembly buildings, warehouses and tool and dye shops. Ford, Jr., wanted more than dark, disintegrating, outdated factories and brown fields. He could have put a fence around the whole River Rouge Complex, bought another marsh and started again, never looking back at the devastation. Instead, he chose a visionary new habitat for fuel-efficient cars of the Solar Age.

In their design, McDonough honored the triangle of 3 E's, first attending to the needs of workers, designers, specialists and management, as well as the executive employers. Together, they created a central brainstorming area: the "Rouge Room" (or the war or peace room) for working ideas. Documents with huge labels were posted on the walls so that everyone could be part of the process of redesigning—with both new thoughts and critical skepticism. The company had already monitored environmental concerns and recognized that the initial costs for the change would be huge—more than for an old model eco-efficient plant. However, they believed that, in time, their investment would more than justify their gamble, their design decision.

The next challenge was how to treat the polluted soil of the brown fields; not just to clean it, but to make it healthy enough to support new trees and grasses and attract wildlife. Company actions included taking all the old soil from the field and bringing in the new. Then they replanted trees and grasses. The cleanup for storm waters would involve eight million dollars in expensive new concrete pipes and treatment plants. They, instead, constructed grass roofs on the buildings and porous parking lots to absorb most of the water. As a result, the runoff was guttered to seep into carefully constructed ditches leading to a newly constructed purification marsh.

By judicious management of the sun, wind and fresh air, the buildings themselves emulated the cherry tree model designed

Henry Ford's River Rouge factory, the largest manufacturing facility in the world, c. 1915.

The good building is not one that hurts the landscape, but one which makes the landscape more beautiful than it was before the building was built.

FRANK LLOYD WRIGHT

to cleanse and lighten, as well as to insulate. In recognition of these new designs this new River Rouge Complex is dedicated to restoration and replenishment of the natural world around it and to creation of a supportive atmosphere for its workers. How wise that was! While many of Detroit's other car manufacturers were being hobbled by their own lack of imagination and foresight, the Ford Motor Company was paying off its initial debts and earning profits.

The future belongs to those who under-stand that doing more with less is compassionate, prosperous and enduring and thus more intelligent, even competitive.

PAUL HAWKEN

McDonough and Braungart believe that, if our future is designed so that everything can be reused or designed afresh, factored in must be the costs of transformation and the long-range benefits of restoring world health and diversity, intelligence and abundance.

* * * * *

Such changes are beginning to happen. People need not only to hear these new voices, but to become them. Because the people of the world are on the edge of the Earth's survival, they must build a bridge of enlightenment, a bridge to a true understanding of nature. People must find out how to work with the Earth, to co-create a new world of re-enchantment and caring. Back in the days of ancient mythologies, different aspects of the human psyche were represented by gods and goddesses. In most of these, the Earth is recognized as the feminine principle, as Mother. To the Greeks she was Gaea, mother of the Titans and the human race. Later she became provider and nurturer of agriculture: Demeter, Ceres to the Romans.

In these days, more and more people are calling Mother Earth, Gaia. Many people feel she is a living force. She is freeing the feminine spirit of compassion and of the Buddhist Tara. She is the new creative force in all living beings. She is nurtured by the sun, related to the stars, Mother to each of us.

Most immediate is Gaia's voice in multiple tones and octaves. It is heard in the profound depth and poignancy of the whale song, in the ultrasonic cries of migrants from the rainforests, singing of a million insects, fish, or crustaceans, birds, the roars of waterfalls or oceans, the mute pleas from the broken rock of open pit mines, the chorales of Earth's flowers. So, listen to these songs with your imaginations, your hearts, your blood and bones and your hands. Listen, and BE.

The seed-keepers are our youth, our children. These are the buds, the leaves and blossoms. These young voices are often hidden—as are the songs of minorities, past and present, and indigenous people —overshadowed by majority ambitions and opinions. Yet they spring up like mushrooms after the

first healing rains. Children hold the strength of humanity to survive. They incorporate mankind's clarity of purpose to live, to reproduce and to create in the face of all obstacles.

It lies with the young people of this nation whether or not it is going to go on to a finish in any wise worthy of its beginning.

- Jane Addams

Let there be no misunderstanding! The voices of the universe are speaking! We ignore them at our own peril!

Children are the world's most valuable resource and its best hope for the future.
PRESIDENT JOHN F. KENNEDY

FINAL WORDS

*If I find a green
meadow splashed
with daisies and
sit down beside
a clear-running
brook, I have
found medicine. It
soothes my hurts as
well as when I sat
in my mother's lap
in infancy, because
the Earth really is
my mother, and
the green meadow
is her lap.*

DEEPAK CHOPRA

CONCLUSION

Writing this book, I have learned many things: First of all, the soul of the garden connects us to the universe through a radiance of light, a rainbow of primal colors, of absolute beauty. These colors are manifested in the full bloom of flowers. They are also in the opening buds of new leaves; in the dazzling reflections of sky; water lilies, kingfishers and damsel flies in lakes and rivers; the brilliance of stones under waves; the iridescent spider web, or threads of dust caught in the sun. They are also in the smiles on the wings of butterflies and in answering smiles in our hearts.

Secondly, I have learned to envision inner gardens: to find in them a climate of pure beauty, leading to a place of jeweled light for discovering the many layers of healing—including prayer. We must concentrate on nurturing new seeds of strength and wisdom. Furthermore, I have learned that we must prepare the soil, teach ourselves and our young the ground of trust and caring needed to hold the rich water and sun.

Thirdly, I have learned that we must honor visionaries. These are the beings working to promote progressive thinking in institutions, perceptions of wholeness, knowledge of our holographic existence as an integral part of the universe. These are not only the great leaders of the world, the Dalai Lamas, Mother Theresas, the Abraham Lincolns of today and yesterday, but also the many leaders of vision, both neighbors and foreigners, who teach through their acts of compassion and wisdom. These visionary qualities also live in each of us, and they are there to be discovered.

Finally, we have need for groups of individuals welded together as one to form communities of healing. The goal of such a mission may be as grand as forming the United Nations; it may be as simple as cooking a meal together or making a garden made sacred by the devotion given to it.

I have learned that such community groups are forming everywhere. They are no longer hierarchical and share equal power, often moving spontaneously in a combined action, more like flocks of birds or schools of fish. There is always a leader, but his or her strength seems to derive more from sharing than from commanding. They behave more like today's Tibetan lamas, who protect their mission and heritage from their Chinese invaders in caves known only to them, or, when imprisoned, they often quietly pray to convert their captors. Underground guerilla fighting almost requires this kind of collaboration, of integrity. When people understand their role in the entire cosmos and so are attuned to a more cosmic reality, their individual decisions begin to correspond to a common good. This creates synchronous, harmonious actions that do not require a chain of command. It is exactly what the brainstorming center at the River Rouge Plant encourages—joint participation, less ego, mission accomplished.

While writing this book, I recalled just such an experience long ago in Boston. A group of college students and I, as artist-director, had a chance to do a mural with kids of that neighborhood. We had been given the whole side of a garage, freshly painted white for the mural. That night, the wall was begun. No daring design, no Picasso-like motivation, but huge-lettered graffiti—at least six names emblazoned five feet high from one end to another. When I first saw it I thought: Horrors! And, of course, the younger kids wanted to emulate it. All of the children were grinning as they carefully spelled out their identities.

So, together, the college kids and I began to fill with colors the spaces around those names—no

To cherish what remains of the Earth, and to foster its renewal, is our only legitimate hope of survival.
WENDELL BERRY

The ultimate test of man's conscience may be his willingness to sacrifice something today for future generations whose words of thanks will not be heard.

GAYLORD NELSON

planning, no color schemes, just painting—and we began grinning, too—what else to do?

By the third night, some faces were added. And, here and there, a dog or pigeon, as well as dozens more names. The loud colors began to dance to their own music, too, moving in every direction on their own initiative—yet—somehow beginning to work in relation to other colors, an unexpected harmony. These primary reds and blues outlined the names carefully so that each seemed to sing separately, and then they began to talk to each other. Finally, a kind of rainbow mosaic reached out across the wall, leaving some white at the top.

It was finished. In these kids' anonymous lives, lost within a city housing project, this was what they wanted to say: "We are here! We are alive! Look, you can see us!" It was their mural—the result of joint participation, absence of ego and lots of passion.

Finally, I have learned to listen to Earth's cries—her songs, her mantras. These belong to each of us as individuals, as communities, as nations and as voting members of our respective governments. Supporting planet Earth is our collective business. It is also our joint responsibility to honor this awakening knowledge of our sacred garden. We have the imagination, the tools and motivation to create in the names of our children and grandchildren, new gardens everywhere in place of devastation.

Our Sacred Garden, the Earth, will be their legacy.

EPILOGUE

We were told by the creator: this is your land.
Keep it for me until I come back.

– Thomas Banyaca, Hopi elder

Across the nation winds of change are fanning a revolutionary campaign. Billions are being poured into clean technology, more efficient buildings and renewable energy. From the Navajo Nation in Arizona to New England—in many towns and cities—wind farms and solar factories and parks are springing up; corporations are building electric vehicles and launching wave power projects.

By purchasing ecologically friendly products, people are changing their habits, and they are gathering in small groups, at schools, libraries, parks and city halls to plan sustainable futures. Indeed, such changes have begun to bond people from coast to coast more emotionally with the land.

This new attentiveness is a reminder that there's more to land than just its economic value. There's beauty and history, for it is the ground which holds the graves of those who have gone before—our ancestors, tribal members, politicians and pioneers—not forgetting the vast Great Plains, its grasslands, its crops, the animal trails pioneers followed west. It was the land that formed the banks and channels of rivers and streams that carried water across the continent. To walk on the land is to feel that very past,

To cherish what remains of the Earth, and to foster its renewal, is our only legitimate hope of survival.
WENDELL BERRY

and to see and sense the remnants of oceans, sea monsters, dinosaurs and great birds.

Arising from this new consciousness about the land itself and about abused and battered landscapes is renewed dedication to the land, or, in the words of Barry Lopez, "redemption through an expression of love."

Also in the winds are the insistent words of California scientist and inventor, Dr. Saul Griffith: "Our most urgent need is not some scientific breakthrough; no, it is for a vast, unprecedented transformation of human behavior."

– James Bishop, Jr., and Bennie Blake

GLOWING MOUNTAIN

184

APPENDIX

Paintings of my children from their youth

Clockwise from left: Antoine, Pierre, Jacques, Jeanne and Dorée, each at a different stage in life.

From Part I, Chapter Two
Personal Awakening to the Sacred

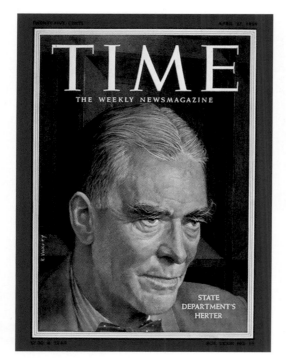

TIME magazine, April 27, 1959 issue

Father — Christian A. Herter served first as Speaker of the House in Massachusetts, then as a congressman from Boston and later as governor (1956—1960). He became Undersecretary of State under John Foster Dulles and eventually Secretary of State under President Dwight Eisenhower. Under John Kennedy, the seventh president he served, he was appointed the first United States Trade Representative.

My father entered the political arena as a man who chose public life. But he should have been a diplomat, since he brought statesmanlike integrity and purpose into his service. As secretary to Herbert Hoover, he helped to provide food for a devastated Europe after World War I. Following World War II, he headed the congressional committee that turned the Marshall Plan into a reality.

From Part II, Chapter Six
Drew Hyde

Drew Hyde became coordinator of Visual Arts for Summerthing. He had an extraordinary sense of timing and knowledge of exactly what was needed where—a truckload of materials carried to an empty city lot for a garden here or scaffolding and paints necessary for murals (often 20 or 30 feet high) there. He understood logistics of each event. Drew Hyde's organizational gifts later earned him the position of Executive Director of Boston's Institute for Contemporary Art. While there, he initiated art programs for high school students around the city and organized the first citywide Earth Festival.

From Part II, Chapter Seven
Visionaries & Transformers

Julie Stone is an extraordinary innovator, gifted ceramicist, always a gardener, and now a planner and photographic record keeper of Boston gardens. She works with the "Boston Schoolyard Initiative " program. Their aim is to transform the disintegrating concrete courtyards and playgrounds surrounding old school buildings into multi-colored gardens, exciting playgrounds and teaching areas. When such an initiative is finished, there is also a transformation of morale for all students and adults involved. The difference these created places of beauty make in the general school atmosphere helps the learning process, and is healing.

Julie's desire is to bring nature back into the lives of urban people, to connect us all again with the living, natural world.

From Part II, Chapter Eight
Lily Yeh and the Village of Arts & Humanities

In 2002, **Lily Yeh** was awarded a leadership grant by the Ford Foundation, all of which she gave to the Village of Arts & Humanities. She felt that enough of a good base had been established so that the village would be able to build wisely with this grant, and she could go freely to help, to paint about freedom in other parts of the world.

Going back to China to visit her filmmaker son, Lily was inspired by the barefoot itinerant artists who visited poor villages, painting and giving hope, to call her newest organization "Barefoot Artists." Currently, she is revisiting Rwanda in Africa to bring the desolate survivors of a 1984 genocidal war not only hope through painting, but encouragement to rebuild their broken houses and fragile lives.

She plans additional trips to Iran on a peacemaking visit and to the Hopis in Arizona as a consultant.

From Part III, Chapter Twelve
Gardens for Humanity

Aimee Beth Ward is a powerhouse! She sculpts, gardens, shoots photos, makes videos and performs. She has exhibited her award winning creations in Arizona, New Mexico and Washington State.

A multi-talented and passionate artist and teacher, Aimee Beth not only inspires her students but empowers them to make their own art and try their hands at gardening. The result? The children develop confidence and pride in their creations—and in themselves.

GRAND CANYON RAPIDS

BIBLIOGRAPHY

Artress, Dr. Lauren. *Walking a Sacred Path, Rediscovering the Labyrinth as a Spiritual Tool.* New York: Riverhead Books, 1995.

Bache, Christopher M.. *The Living Classroom: Teaching and Colllective Consciousness.* Albany, New York: State University of New York, 2008.

Bateson, Gregory. *Mind and Nature: A Necessary Unity.* New York: Bantam Books, 1980.

Becker, Robert O.. *Cross Currents: The Perils of Electropollution, The Promise of Electromedicine.* New York: G. P. Putnam's Sons, 1990.

Berry, Thomas. *The Dream of the Earth.* Sierra Club Books, 1988.

_____. *The Great Work, Our Way into the Future.* Bell Tower, 1999.

_____. *Evening Thoughts.* Sierra Club Books, 2006.

_____. *The Christian Future and the Fate of the Earth.* Maryknoll, New York: Orbis Books, 2009.

Berry, Wendell. *Bringing It To The Table.* Berkley, California: Counterpoint, 2009.

Collins, Andrew. *The New Circlemakers, Insights into the Crop Circle Mystery.* Virginia Beach, Virginia: 4th Dimension Press, 1992.

Devereux, Paul. *Earth Memory: Sacred Sites — Doorways to Earth's Mysteries.* St. Paul, Minnesota: Llewellyn Publications, 1992.

Edwards, Andres R.. *The Sustainability Revolution.* Gabriola Island, B.C. Canada: New Society Publishers, 2005.

Eiseley, Loren. *The Star Thrower.* New York: A Harvest Book, Harcourt, Inc., Random House, 1978.

Ferguson, Marilyn. *The Aquarian Conspiracy.* J.P. Tarcher, Inc. 1980.

Fleischman, Paul. *Seedfolks.* New York: Harper Trophy, Joanna Cotler Books, 1997.

Gablik, Suzie. *The Re-enchantment of Art.* New York: Thames and Hudson, 1991.

Gore, Al. *An Inconvient Truth*. Rodale Press, 2006.

Hamilton, Vijali. *World Wheel: One Woman's Quest for Peace*. Castle Valley, Utah: World Wheel Press, 2007.

Hathaway, Mark and Boff, Leonardo. *The Tao of Liberation, Exploring the Ecology of Transformation*. Maryknoll, New York: Orbis Books, 2009.

Hynez, H. Patricia. *A Patch of Eden*. White River Junction, Vermont: America's Inner-City Gardeners, Chelsea Green Publishing Company.

Johnson, Lady Bird. *Wildflowers Across America*. Artabras/Abbeville Press, 1993.

Kingsolver, Barbara. *Prodigal Summer*. New York: Harper Perennial, 2000.

_____. *Animal, Vegetable, Miracle*.

Lanza, Patricia. *Lasagna Gardening*. Rodale Press, 1998.

Laszlo, Ervin. *WorldShift 2012*. Rochester, Vermont: Inner Traditions, 2009.

Lovelock, James E.. *Gaia: A New Look at Life on Earth*. Oxford, UK: Oxford University Press, 1979.

also: *Healing Gaia: Practical Medicine for the Planet*. New York: Harmony Books, 1991.

Macy, Joanna. *World as Lover, World as Self*. Berkeley, California: Parallel Press, 1991.

Martin, Michele. *Music in the Sky, The Life, At, and Teachings of the 17th Gyalwa Karmapa Ogyen Trinley Dorje*. Boudler, Colorado: Snow Lion Publications, 2003.

McDonough, William, and Braungart, Michael. *Cradle to Cradle*. New York: Northpoint Press, Division of Farrar, Straus & Giroux, 2002.

Mollison, Bill. *Permaculture*. Washington, DC: Island Press, 1990.

Sheldrake, Rupert. *The Presence of the Past: Morphic Resonance and the Habits of Nature*. New York: Random House, 1988.

_____. *The Rebirth of Nature, The Greening of Science and God*. New York: Bartam Books, 1991.

Wharton, Charles Heizer, Ph.D.. *Ten Thousand Years from Eden*. Orlando, Florida: Winmark Publishing, 2001.

Williams, Terry Tempest. *Finding Beauty in a Broken World*. New York: Pantheon Books, 2008.

Wilson, E.O.. *The Creation*. New York: W. W. Norton & Co Inc.

Wright, Michaelle Small. *Behaving As If the God in All LIfe Mattered: A New Age Ecology*. Jeffersonton, Virginia: Perelandra, Lmtd, 1983.

_____. *Perelandra Garden Workbook, 2nd Edition*. Jeffersonton, Virginia: Perelandra, Lmtd, 1993.

ABOUT THE AUTHOR

Gardens have been an enduring part of Adele Seronde's life since she was a child in New England. Born in 1925, the daughter of a statesman father, artist mother, and grandparents who were all fervent gardeners, she spent many childhood weekends on the family farm learning how to plant, weed and harvest flowers and crops. Her father's words during those early years still ring in her ears: "If you have ideas, you are responsible for bringing them to life."

That advice and those early gardens have been the force behind many of Adele's life's accomplishments as a poet, painter, mother, grandmother and community activist, all the while creating gardens of her own, and weaving nature's colors into her poetry and paintings.

The idea for this book began to germinate in 1987, when Adele joined a group on a tour to visit the Chalice Gardens in Glastonbury, England. So profoundly moved was she by the meaning and beauty of the Chalice Well that she felt her lifetime of loving nature had crystallized into a mission: to help emulate and create such gardens of the spirit around the world and to create this book of paintings, photos, poetry and text. The essence of this book is to show how gardens of the spirit can grow through the hearts and hands of enlightened communities.

Meantime, in 1995, she started Gardens for Humanity, based in Sedona, Arizona, which is still flourishing and has spurred the creation of community gardens across the U.S. In her heart, Seronde believes that today more and more people are awakening to new love—and responsibility—for our sacred garden, the Earth.

Other books available from
SANCTUARY PUBLICATIONS

ISBN: 9780984375424 ✦ 232 pages ✦ $22.95

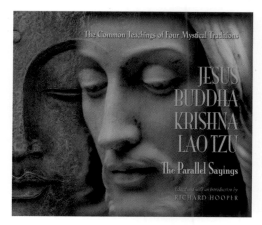

ISBN: 9780978533496 ✦ 200 pages ✦ $22.95